At Last I Know
My Father

At Last I Know My Father

Through letters found sixty-three years
after he was killed in action in World War II

Mary Cameron Betancourt

INFINITE *Light* PRESS

Florida

ISBN 978-0-9856973-5-8

Infinite Light Press, Imprint Division
One Infinite Light, Inc.
1037 Stone Lake Drive
Ormond Beach, Florida 32174

www.infinitelightpress.com
www.oneinfinitelight.com

Because I have had a life long desire to know my dad, I wish to dedicate this book to him and my mom, and to my wonderful Lord who made it all possible.

Psalm 37:4 "Delight yourself also in the Lord, and He shall give you the desires of your heart." NKJ

COMMENTS FROM READERS

"I am an avid reader and at age 43 I did not think a book could be so powerful as to bring me to tears, but that is what your book did. You really brought to life a great American hero. The love he had for your mom is beautiful. It is clear through the letters that he loved her with every ounce of his heart." BILLY C. OF DERRY, NEW HAMPSHIRE

"This is an amazing story—a time capsule! I'm still speechless, and I feel as though we were all there with your mom and dad as the story unfolded. From family stories I knew three things about your dad: that he was a great guy, he was quite the athlete, and that he once rode a bicycle up a flight of stairs. After reading your book I have to add a fourth fact in that he was an amazing man! I am proud to be his nephew!" DAN T., BRIDGEWATER, MASSACHUSETTS

"Those letters became a window to the past: historically: the military life and battlegrounds; spiritually: your dad showed his beliefs and trusted the Lord; romantically: how beautiful was their courtship, and the funny things, too! How he loved you, your mom, his family, church, his country, and fellow soldiers. It's a timeless story!" ANA Y., KALISPELL, MONTANA

"Their letters were a precious part of our history." LYNN W., PALM COAST, FLORIDA

Comments From Readers

"For years, every Monday morning I counted the weekly collection at church with your mother and Theresa. I remember your mother telling me that the night she met your father she and Mary had plans to go to the Old Orchard Beach pier. Their father did not tell them not to go, but he pointed out that it could be dangerous because the shores were being watched. As a result, they changed their plans and went to the club where she met your father." BEA R., SACO, MAINE

"The story I remember from my mother was when your future parents came to Biddeford for their pre-marriage blood tests, they stopped in at our home to say, 'Hello.' I was about six months old and was in a bad way as teeth were pushing through. Your father walked the floor with me until I stopped fussing." REV. ALBERT C., LIMERICK, MAINE

"I can remember visiting your mom and couldn't understand why she never remarried, but I always held her in highest regards as a Cameron. Now I understand better the true and beautiful relationship they had. I couldn't imagine living in those days. Your parents were the prime example of true love." ED C., ALLENSTOWN, NEW HAMPSHIRE

"Memorial Day was more significant to me because of your book." NELLE M., SWANTON, OHIO

"The gift that you leave the reader is truly life-changing." KRISTI B., LOCK HAVEN, PENNSYLVANIA

Comments From Readers

"*This book touched me in several different ways. My daddy was in WWII, but he never talked about anything. I wonder if he went through a lot of things your dad went through: hunger, no water, no way to clean or wash hands, no sleep, danger, and all the things he mentioned. So it made me feel as though I know what Daddy went through.*"
LINDA B. OF CROSS LANES, WEST VIRGINIA

"*Toward the end when your father describes the situation those men were enduring, tears came to my eyes as I could see that your father was losing strength and he so wanted to go home.*" SISTER THERESE O., COLORADO SPRINGS, COLORADO

"*Many of the women [I met] were mourning the deaths of their spouses who had served in WWII. I don't have those stories in my family. Your book will continue my understanding of how war affected the lives of so many people.*"
SISTER FRANCES B. OF LA CROSSE, WISCONSIN

"*Your book is a deterrent to war. It is the best book I have read about WWII.*" PEGGY SUE R., TELLURIDE, COLORADO

"*The place that was the most moving [on a visit to Normandy, France] was the cemetery with thousands of markers--each one someone's son or brother or husband or all of the above. I am so glad you got to see your dad's grave. I do remember you going to Europe with your grandparents so many years ago; but, of course, I didn't know your special secret.*" CATHY L., OLD ORCHARD BEACH, MAINE

Table of Contents

FOREWARD

Rarely have I been so affected by a book as I have this one, a rare and touching tribute by a daughter to the father she never had the privilege of knowing. That is, until Mary Cameron Betancourt came into possession of letters written between her father, Gerard Cameron, and his wife Frances from the time they met, through his service in World War II where he was sadly killed in battle. Then, at last, Mary knew her father through his words—a wonderfully warm and loving man with an abiding devotion to his wife, his baby daughter, and his country.

This book offers a unique perspective of mid-twentieth century life in America, the soldiers of World War II who fought gallantly in foreign lands to defend freedom and democracy, and the families on the homefront who supported them and prayed for their return. *At Last I Know My Father* is a compelling story that is nostalgic, poignant, heartrending —yet also sweet and tremendously moving. In addition, it is a chronicle of the rapid maturing by circumstance of two lovestruck twenty-year-olds. Readers will be absorbed by this very personal and tender account of one couple's journey through the war years.

Many thanks to Mary for letting me contribute to this extraordinary project by designing the cover and the layout and helping to publish this book. I feel very blessed for the experience of getting to know Mary, her father, and her mother in such an intimate way.

Liane France, Author and Publisher, 2014
www.infinitelightpress.com

THE PURPOSE OF THIS BOOK is to give honor to the wonderful Lord who created me and to my very special parents: Frances Barbara Colpitts and Gerard Edward Cameron.

My mother, widowed the day before her twenty-fourth birthday, loved me unconditionally and sacrificially. She and my father hoped to have a large family. I would have been the oldest child, but ended up being the only one.

Loving me intensely, as a mother in such a position would, she rejoiced in my successes, was disappointed over my failures, and heartbroken over my mistakes. Like our loving Lord, she never rejected me and chose to love me still.

My father was killed in World War II. He had four days leave when I was born. He brought my mother and me home from the hospital. Within a month, he was on a troop ship headed first to North Africa and then to Italy.

Consequently, I became a World War II war orphan. There was always a hole in my heart, and growing up I realized that I was different because I only had one parent and no brothers and sisters. My parents were both from families of eight children. Except for one other fatherless family, I realized that all my cousins had fathers and that almost all my classmates had fathers, brothers, and sisters. Why didn't I?

My mother and I were blessed to have a home with her parents and my mom's younger sister Theresa who was like a big sister to me. They were always very good to us. My father's parents and siblings were always kind and loving to my mother and to me. I am so thankful for all the relatives on both sides. Many of them told me about my father, but I always longed to know him personally. Had his life been spared, how different would my life have been?

In 2007, a year after my mom joined him in heaven, a cousin's spouse was cleaning out my mother's house. He had been told to take everything to the dump as nothing of value was left. He called my Aunt Theresa and told her that he had found something she should see: a box of all my father's letters from the time my parents met until his death. How grateful I am that this treasure has been entrusted to me. At last I know my father!

In 2009, a cousin of mine was cleaning out my father's sister's house. She found another treasure: five compositions my father had written when he was in high school. Two of them were dated 1933. I have included four of them in this work. These also have been entrusted to me thanks to my Aunt Ginny and cousin Lisa Rogers.

Thus, this book is born. I don't want my father, who sacrificed his life for my freedom and for yours, to be forgotten.

ACKNOWLEDGMENTS

WHEN I RECEIVED the box of letters in 2007, almost immediately I realized that I had to write this book. As I read my father's letters, I knew what the title had to be. Over the past five years, I have changed jobs, been unemployed, kept a vigil at my husband's side through two different surgeries, and tried to keep house along with writing this book and editing the letters. I thank my husband for his patience with me. I'm sure he wondered if I would ever finish this project.

I am grateful to Mr. William Cummins, author and publisher; Susan Joiner, author, former journalist, friend and next door neighbor; and my cherished cousin Peggy Sue Richards, retired librarian; for their much appreciated suggestions and encouragement.

Many thanks to Sandy Bennett, a retired English teacher and friend, for the many hours of her precious time spent in correcting my many mistakes and offering her wise advice.

My father's brother Joe Cameron, who entered eternal rest in February 2012, delighted me in recalling his recollections of my dad. His brother Bill Cameron, who entered Glory on his ninety-third birthday in 2013, also shared some of his memories with me. My Aunt Theresa, my mom's younger sister, was most encouraging and helpful.

Special thanks to my dear friend Carol Cline for her obedience to the Lord in assisting me.

Joe Rosa, a friend and neighbor, was very helpful with preparing a CD of pictures and documents.

Thanks to my cousin Terry Pease Walker for information about grants. Unfortunately, I didn't qualify for one!

The revision of this book would not have been possible without author and publisher Liane France of Infinite Light Press. Liane has offered her valuable time and expertise to enhance this book and raise it to a new level. She has understood my passion to bring honor to my parents, and she has done everything she possibly could to help me achieve this. I am eternally grateful to her. She has become my sister and friend.

To my many relatives, friends, and acquaintances who kept saying, "How is your book coming along?" I say thank you for not giving up on me! At last it's done!

CHAPTER ONE

Family History and Settings

M Y FATHER, GERARD EDWARD CAMERON, was born August 16, 1918 in Boston, Massachusetts. His dad, William D. Cameron, was the son of a Gloucester fisherman of Scottish descent. His mom, Jennie Joyce Cameron, was from south Boston of Irish descent. They were a very close knit, devout Catholic family who made their home in North Quincy, Massachusetts, where they raised their eight children in a large two story house on West Squantum Street across the street from a golf course.

Six of the eight children: Joe, Gerry, Ginny, Jim, Bill, and Margie

The following compositions my father wrote in high school reveal how family oriented he was.

"An Incident of My Childhood"

Sometime during the time I was four years of age my father had purchased an automobile. This was the first one that my father had owned. Not knowing how to drive, he had to be taught by an instructor. When the instructor had come to do his part, I begged my father to let me go along with him.

The first thing I did was to watch everything the instructor did which taught me something about the way the car was operated.

The next morning I went straight to the car, played around for a while, then thought I wanted a ride. Having much confidence in myself, I decided to make the automobile go. First I meddled with the transmission until it moved. Feeling that the car was ready to go, I then stepped on the self starter. The desired effect had come and I was making the automobile go backwards. As I was doing this, my frightened mother came running from the house and caught me just in time from going over an embankment.

That afternoon my brother and I were playing around the house and my brother wanted a drink. I, not wanting one, was too lazy to go and get him one. As a result, I came upon an old rusty can which I thought contained water. My brother, then two years old, drank the contents of the can and found it to be gasoline instead of water. To this day he always blames anything that is the matter with him on the gasoline that I let him drink.

This unfortunate brother was my Uncle Bill. I asked him if he recalled the story of this incident and he said no. However, my Uncle Joe, a younger brother, remembered this story circulating throughout the years among the family.

"My Home"

Anyone stepping into my home would find several young children who are always found together. When one of them goes upstairs, the others always go along with him.

In the morning all are in the kitchen because it is time to again fill up the part of our bodies which must not be forgotten. When breakfast is over, most of the family is preparing to go to school or go to work.

The usual questions, "Where is my hat?" or "Where is my book?' usually arise , and poor Mother is always the one who has to find the different belongings. She is greatly relieved when most of us are gone for the day.

After the long school day, the pantry is visited most. The result is that when Mother is preparing for supper, she has no supper to prepare. One of us has to pay the penalty by making a visit to the store.

During the supper hour, all the happenings of the long day are discussed. Then comes the job of doing the dishes, a job which is done by all.

After supper the radio is the most interesting thing with which to pass the evening. So it is on most of the evening which makes studying a difficult task.

By the time my Uncle Joe came along, my grandmother had found a solution to the raiding of her pantry after school by her hungry children. Just as they came through the door, she would pull a pan of hot biscuits out of the oven for the after school snack and thus save her supper from being devoured prematurely.

"An Interesting Member of My Family"

Some people are very unfortunate in some ways when it comes to having brothers and sisters. I happen to be fortunate having several of each who are always wanting me to help them with something, or make something, or play with them.

One of my brothers is a very interesting little boy who seems to care only for something to eat and play. We call him "Bob" a name which seems to fit him well.

One day as I was putting on the three year old tot's shoes he told me that his shoes were just like a cow. This made me wonder why. So I asked him. The answer was, "Because they have long tongues."

To visit our grandmother is what Bob always wants to do because he knows that she will give him a cookie. This is one of his weaknesses. Whenever he is at Grandmother's, he is always to be found right next to the cookie tin, and cannot be taken away until he has had his fill.

When Mother is working around the house, Bob is the one that looks after the baby. He seems to do a fine job of it.

My Uncle Joe was two years older than Bob and remembered him well. Bob was rather precocious. The family had their meals together family style. The rule was: take as much as you want, but you must eat everything you take. Uncle Joe remembered Bob cleaning his plate and my grandmother asking him if he'd had enough.

He replied, "No, I'm not plugged up yet!"

When this little brother Bob was four years old, he and a baby brother named Leo contracted whooping cough, measles, and pneumonia all at the same time. They both died in the same week and their funeral was the same day. My grandmother often told me how sad it was to see the two small caskets side by side. Another child, my Aunt Margie,(mother of fourteen children), was sick at the same time with the same three illnesses, and was not expected to live, but through God's mercy and grace, she lived.

My grandmother told me, that at the time of the loss of the two children, my father told her that if he arrived in Heaven before the rest of the family, he would pray very hard for everyone to get there. Did he have a premonition that he would be the next child to pass on?

" A Vacation Experience"

Gerard Cameron 304, English 9–1

April 28, 1933

Washington is one of the cities I have vacationed in. I consider this city the most beautiful place I have ever seen. If one should ask me what to do for a vacation, I would make Washington my first and best suggestion. One could stay there a year and do nothing but go sightseeing and not see everything there is to see.

It was a hot summer late afternoon when I reached my uncle's house. The first thing anyone would want to do in my condition would be to cool off. This made my uncle suggest a midnight fishing trip which is a common thing for the residents of Washington to do because they are so handy to Chesapeake Bay. It takes only an hour to go from the heart of the government city to the best fishing grounds around that section of the country.

The time seemed to pass very slowly until I reached the boat. Then I was contented and cooled by the water and cool breezes.

Just as our little party was all prepared to take up anchor, after a very fine fishing trip, a bad gale swept over the bay until every boat was tossing in a grand style. Following this came a thunderstorm which made me feel as if we would never get back to land safely.

If anyone wants a thrilling experience, just get in Chesapeake Bay in a small boat when there is a bad thunderstorm and so dark you can't see ten feet before you. Try it some time.

My dad graduated from North Quincy High School in 1936. While a student there, he played in the orchestra and band, played football, and was co-captain of the wrestling team. In 1936 he became the State Wrestling Champion in the 155 pound class.

GERARD E. CAMERON
"Gerry"

318 West Squantum St., Montclair

Varsity Football '34, '35; Varsity Wrestling '34, '35, '36, Co-captain; Hi-Y Club '35, '36; Varsity Club '35, '36; Orchestra '34, '35; Band '34, '35, '36; Traffic Squad '35, '36; 1936 State Wrestling Champion in 155 lb. class

Wrestling

Coached by Frank E. MacDonald, the wrestling team had an excellent season, winning five matches and losing two. The matches lost were very close, however, each being decided by a single bout.

Paced by Co-Captains "Gerry" Cameron and "Tommy" Coleman, the team won the Massachusetts Interscholastic Wrestling Championship for the second successive year, and the Tufts Athletic Association awarded the team a large silver cup. "Tony" DelGallo will be wrestling captain for the 1937 season.

My dad was an avid bicyclist, and while in high school, he had his own bicycle repair business in the basement of the family home.

*Gerry Cameron, the only high school senior
to advertise his own business in the yearbook!*

He also formed a cycle club and became its president, entering bicycle races throughout New England. By winning the mile race trials, he qualified for the national race in Chicago in 1940. After graduation, his business had grown enough for him to move it into a shop.

In March 2008, my dad's youngest living brother, Uncle Joe came to Florida for a delightful visit. One day I asked him if he had any memories of my father that revealed his character—he did.

On one occasion, there happened to be a bicycle race which went right by the corner of West Squantum Street where my dad lived. My grandfather and Uncle Joe went to watch the race in support of my father. They saw many guys on racing bikes whiz by. Finally along came my dad on a regular bike holding another racer's bike which had a flat tire. My dad asked my grandfather to find the guy a good tire. Then my dad joined the race and won!

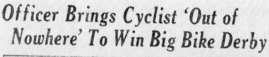

Officer Brings Cyclist 'Out of Nowhere' To Win Big Bike Derby

Following the finish of the 20-mile round-the-city bicycle derby last evening, LeRoy Ryan was right on the job to snap the winner, the runner-up and the third placer. The winner was Gerard Cameron, wearing numeral 6, of Montclair who covered the distance in 1h 4m 25s. Second only to Cameron was Stanley Beecher, No. 36, also of Ward Six, who negotiated the route in 1h 5m 20s. Third was William Gould, No. 56, of Merrymount, who set the pace more than half way around the circuit. His time was 1h 6m 45s. The race, the first of its kind ever held in Quincy, was sponsored by the WPA Quincy Recreation Project.

Another story spoke to his generous nature. One day Uncle Joe and a friend visited my dad's cycle shop. My dad gave them 30 cents to go across the street to buy each one, including himself, a ten cent ice cream cone.

However, Gerry Cameron's big heart backfired one night when he allowed a homeless man to sleep in his shop. When he opened the shop the next morning, the man was gone, and so was all the money in his cash register. Being a devout Christian, I'm sure my dad quickly forgave the destitute man.

Before enlisting in the United States Army on March 17, 1941, my dad worked for a time in the boiler shop of the Fore River Shipyard in Quincy, Massachusetts. He was the first employee of the boiler shop to enter the service.

My dad received his basic training at Camp Edwards, Massachusetts. Then he was assigned to Saco, Maine where the soldiers' barracks were in a local shoe shop.

Camp Edwards, West Barnstable County, Massachusetts

My mom was born December 10, 1920 in Beverly, Massachusetts to Mary Hickey Colpitts and Garnet F. Colpitts. My maternal grandmother was a twin from Skibbereen, County Cork, Ireland, while my grandfather was born in New Brunswick, Canada, of German-English descent. When my mother was two years old, the family moved to a farmhouse on five acres of land in Saco, Maine. My mother lived in Saco until her death in 2006. My mother was the sixth child in the family with four brothers and one sister older than her and one brother and one sister younger.

First Communion: Frances, Mary, and Bernard Colpitts

Like the Camerons, the Colpitts family was also a devout Catholic family. My mom attended a Catholic elementary school and Thornton Academy in Saco for high school.

She graduated in 1938. She worked one or more summers as a waitress at Grindstone Inn in Winter Harbor on the coast of Maine. Then she worked in an office until I was born. She also taught Sunday school in her local church.

Certain supplies were scarce in the early 1940's and families were given ration stamps for food and gas. My Aunt Theresa told me that my grandmother used to trade stamps with neighbors in order to have the necessary ingredients for cooking and baking. Butter was very scarce and they had to use margarine which was white in color. It came with an orange powder which they mixed in to give it color.

Because of the demands on the food supply during war time, families planted "Victory Gardens." My mom's dad always planted a vegetable garden, but my paternal grandfather had his Victory Garden in his backyard during the war. It was a form of patriotism as well as helping people provide for themselves when food was scarce.

During World War II there were German submarines in the Atlantic off the coast of Maine. This necessitated my father's unit to be stationed there. They patrolled the beaches. There were blackouts at night, so when the loud fire alarm sounded, everyone had to dim their lights, lower their window shades, and create as much darkness as possible. The local textile mills ,which were operating all night, had their windows painted black in order to camouflage their operations.

My mom and her siblings walked to school, work, the stores, the movie theater, and church. If the weather was inclement, they might hire a taxi. Gasoline was scarce, and families did not have much. Usually there was one vehicle per family.

In the evenings, families would gather around the radio as there was no TV, and certainly no computers. Those who played the piano and other instruments would practice and maybe get together for a sing-a-long or jam session. Young people read books and knew how to entertain themselves with checkers, board games, and all kinds of card games.

Such was life in the late 1930's and early 1940's for the Cameron and Colpitts families!

CHAPTER TWO

The Courtship

THE ERA WAS WORLD WAR II. The year was 1942. The date was May 30. The place was Saco, Maine. Because German submarines were cruising in Atlantic waters, the 181st Infantry of the United States Army was utilizing a Saco shoe factory for barracks while they patrolled the beaches.

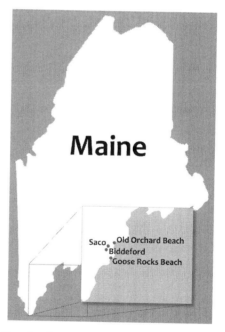

It was a Saturday night. The USO was hosting a dance at the Unity Club for the soldiers in their hall on North Street. A young private Gerard Edward Cameron, nicknamed Gerry, asked a young lady, Mary Colpitts, my aunt, for a dance. He would be twenty-four in August. When he asked her age, she told him she would be twenty-six on June thirteenth. He didn't believe her.

Mary said, "My younger sister is sitting right over there. Ask her."

Mary escorted Gerry to where her sister Frances, my mother, was sitting and introduced them. It was love at first sight for both of them! The remainder of the evening Frances and Gerry spent dancing and becoming acquainted. Frances' blue eyes followed his every move. Gerry couldn't believe this young lady's charm and beauty.

At the end of the evening Gerry asked the two sisters what Mass they would be attending the next day as he had learned they were of the same faith as he.

He turned to Mary and said, "I will have your future husband there."

Mary replied, "I don't need you to do any matchmaking!"

To which Gerry responded, "I think you do. You're almost twenty-six and nothing's happened yet!"

The next morning Mary and Frances were in church when a group of soldiers entered and proceeded to sit directly in front of them. After Mass Gerry introduced Bill Pease to the girls.

He said to Mary, "Meet your future husband," and to Bill, "Meet your future wife."

Both Mary and Bill were embarrassed, especially Bill, since he already had a girlfriend.

The following are segments of correspondence written during my parents' courtship from June 1, 1942 through January 29, 1943—with minor corrections.

The Courtship

From Gerry, June 1, 1942, 5:30 A.M., Saco, Maine

Dear Frances,

It is a most beautiful morning, in fact, the best I've seen yet this year. After having seen you Sunday, I found myself thinking of you a few times, so I thought that there couldn't be anything drastically wrong with writing you a little letter. Here's hoping that you'll be surprised and more or less welcome it.

Gee! It was thrilling to see the little children receive their first communion. Did you have a part in their preparation?

I had left the factory with a hope of seeing you at church. Little did I think I'd be sitting in front of you. As a matter of fact, I didn't really know it until after you and Mary received. [Holy Communion] *However, when I first entered the pew, I had an idea it might possibly have been you who was responsible for that little 'pst' in the pew behind me.*

It must be said that you and Mary made quite an impression on the boys. Your apparel was most impressive. I particularly liked your green hat, bag, and shoes. I told you Saturday I liked your neat coat.

That fellow I introduced to you is one of my better Catholic buddies. He's a fine chap, a few years older than Mary and good interesting company. His birthday is also June thirteenth. What a coincidence! He is particularly interested in gardening. He's already expressed a desire to chat with your father about your garden.

He also enjoys dancing such as was taking place there at the Unity Club. Bowling is another interest.

So it all adds up to this: we are looking forward to enjoying a few hours in company with Mary and you. Whether it will be bowling, dancing, walking, talking, or what have you, doesn't matter. I'm quite certain that every moment will be a pleasure.

Well then, unless we hear differently from you, we shall be looking forward to a rendezvous on either Thursday, Friday, Saturday, or Sunday evening, depending upon whenever we have a pass. Of course, I'll telephone first.

From Gerry, June 8, 1942, Old Orchard Beach, Maine

Dear Frances,

It's a good thing that they gave me a pass Sunday afternoon because I had more or less intended to sneak out to see you Sunday night.

The Courtship

Just think I only looked at my watch once. I'd forgotten all about the time. It's a good thing Bill did or else!

Gee! We hadn't intended to barge in on you at dinnertime. I had thought that you'd have finished dinner before one-thirty. Be sure and especially thank your mother for me. Strawberry shortcake has always been one of my weaknesses. It was a most delightful unexpected treat.

Bill and I took particular notice of you girls giving your mother a hand. That's a very good sign.

Meeting your folks was grand. Already we've taken a great liking to all of them.

Gosh, Fran! I must apologize for not having given you more attention Sunday afternoon. I wanted to, but I was really afraid to look at your eyes, because if you ever looked at me the way you did Saturday night, why, well I'd be more or less overcome, and it wouldn't be the best thing to let everyone see me while in such a condition. What do you think ? Next time I'll make up for it. Wait and see.

Gee! When you look at me, it sure does things to me. What a thrill! Don't ever lose your innocence , because you wouldn't be able to look that way if you did. Every time I close my eyes I can still see you looking up at me.

Frances, you are a real lady. It's swell knowing you. What a lucky guy I am. Little did I even hope to meet anyone anywhere as nice as you are.

Just as soon as we started to run back to the factory, I started looking forward to Wednesday or Thursday night. My hopes are high.

It's probably a good thing that I'm on duty here at the beach and not able to get leave often because I'd undoubtedly be pestering you for dates. I don't want to be a pest. So please don't let me.

What do you say? Would you give Bill and Mary their birthday spanking if I held them? Some coincidence, both on the thirteenth!

It's time to eat. So I'll be waiting to see you, hear you, and read a letter from you.

In the family, a story has been handed down and alluded to in my dad's letters of him picking Aunt Mary up and, with her draped over his shoulder, giving her a birthday spanking as he maneuvered down Tasker Street where the two girls lived. Mr. Colpitts, my grandfather and the two girls dad, stood watching and got a big kick out of it!

My mother's first letter to my dad Gerry was written the same day.

From Frances, June 8, 1942, Saco, Maine

I came back to the office early this noon to write you a letter.

You made quite a hit with the family Sunday — especially Theresa. [Theresa was eleven years old at the time and was very captivated by the budding romances of her two older sisters.]

I owe you an apology for not introducing you to my girlfriend Saturday night. I guess I was too interested in a certain Mr. Cameron.

I think your friend Bill is very nice and I know Mary does too. It was too bad you had to get back so soon. My brother Albert and his family came over just a short time after you left.

Thinking he could get all the gas he wanted working at the Navy yard in Portsmouth, Albert just bought a new Hudson. Now they tell him he has to take the bus and all the gas he can get now is three gallons a week. He had an X card but they called it in. If he had known that would happen, he'd never have bought the new car.

From Gerry, June 12, 1942, Old Orchard Beach, Maine

Dearest Frances,

Today everything has run off ok. This morning we rode out to Goose Rocks Beach and then slept in the woods until ten thirty. Only yours truly didn't do much sleeping. Preferred to think back over Wednesday and Thursday nights. Thanks for everything. I never thought it could happen this way and so to perfection.

At one o'clock we started for here. [Old Orchard Beach] At two I was in the briny water, but it was too cold to stay for more than five minutes. Then more sunburn. By the end of this month, I will be your brown man. My greatest hope for present is that we stay here for the next nine months. You are the reason and I'd detest any thoughts of being deprived of spending a few precious hours of every week with Frances.

I kept one eye open on the beach for Mary and possibly you, but to no avail. Our telescope is back from repair. That should make looking for you an even easier task.

Last night while walking with you, I was supposed to get Bill a birthday card for Mary, but it didn't even enter my brain which was so occupied with my heart's delight. So Bill said that he'd call Mary tonight and orally express his greetings etc. While we are on that subject, please extend my best possible returns of the day to Mary. She is a lot of fun.

When and if you do come down to the beach, pick a spot right opposite the highest part of the roller-coaster track and I'll do my best to be there.

Well I have still to see you leave the house in the morning. That would pep me up all day. [The shoe shop where the soldiers stayed was visible from my grandparents' home.]

Already I'm anxiously looking forward to my next pass. I didn't hear anything from the top kick about being out two nights in a row. But I did get a heck of a ribbing from some of the boys. They're all waiting to get a glimpse of you. You'll open their eyes. My better friends are waiting to meet you. Won't I be proud!

Gee your mother is nice to me. Remember me to her.

From Frances, June 14, 1942, 9:45 P.M., Saco, Maine

I just returned from the show with Mary, Paul, Santa, and her brother Mike. [Santa and Mike were next door neighbors.]

When you called today, I was sound asleep. Maybe I was dreaming?

All the boys I danced with last night wanted to know if I was going to watch them parade today. Theresa went and enjoyed it. If you had been in it, nothing could have kept me from it.

My mother and father are still kidding Mary about getting spanked.

Your Sweetheart,

Frances

From Gerry, June 16, 1942, Old Orchard Beach, Maine

All weekend I'd had my heart set on seeing you tonight, but it just wasn't to be. Anyhow it will help make the next time, tomorrow I hope, I hope, all the more sweeter. Believing that everything happens for the best, one can put up with almost any disappointment.

Sunday afternoon, while walking my post on the beach, I came across Mary, Santa, [neighbors of my mom], *and a tall soldier from the artillery. Santa said she had seen you in church. I asked her how did you look.*

She said, "She looked cute".

I replied, "You ain't kidding!"

Seems as if I've known you for years . . .One of my greatest joys is going to church and praying for you and us.

If you were watching me parade, I'd probably be stepping all over the fellow in front of me. But I'd want you to be there just the same.

What to do Wednesday evening hasn't even entered my head. Just as long as I'm with you, how, when, why, or what fore doesn't matter. Have you any ideas? I'm always open to suggestions.

When I read your closing, my equilibrium was upset in a whirling fashion. Thanks, Sweetheart!

From Gerry, June 21, 1942, Saco, Maine

Today is the first day of summer and it seems all indications tend to make it the very best one of my life. All day I've been happier than ever before. You made me that way. Thanks, Sweetheart. The fellows say that I have a big smile on my face even while I'm sleeping.

Saturday night I was reported A.W.O.L. When I found out about it, the expression on my face didn't even change. I didn't care what happened.

This morning the Captain looked me up. The following conversation resulted.

"Cameron, were you absent for bed check last night?"

"Yes, Sir!"

"Did you go out without a pass?"

"Yes, Sir!"

"I thought you were a better soldier than that!"

The Courtship

"What time did you get in?"

"With the convoy sir."

"Did you come back with the convoy?"

"Yes, Sir!"

"Why did you do it?"

"Well, Sir, my name was on the books to go to the dance from eleven o'clock yesterday morning. At four o'clock I called up my girlfriend and told her that I'd see her at the dance. At seven o'clock I was taking a shower when Sergeant Whelan told the boys I couldn't go. After my getting all cleaned up and dressed up, the sergeant came to me and told me that I couldn't go. I said I was going just the same and I did go. I had to stand up the girlfriend two nights this week and I wasn't going to do so last night."

"Is this girl from Biddeford?"

"No, Sir!"

"Saco?"

"Yes, Sir!"

"French?"

"No!! Sir!"

"Irish?"

"Yes, Sir!"

"Blonde?"

"No, Sir!"

"Brunette?"

"Yes, Sir!"

"Blue eyes?"

"Blue gray , Sir!"

"Are you going to marry her?"

"Never can tell, Sir!"

That was all. Then he went to Sergeant Smart, my sergeant at the beach, and said, "Do you think we should confine him for thirty days?"

The serge said, "No, Sir. He's in love!"

Then the captain gave a big smile. All the time he was questioning me he could hardly keep a straight face. So I don't think anything will happen. You know, first offense and not too serious a one.

Several fellows saw and heard the whole affair. They asked me if it was worth it. I said, "And how! I'd do it all over again."

Frances, I just couldn't have stood you up last night. Last night topped all so far. I'm in a different world. I can't even write right!

Tonight I hope to get to church again....I've an awful lot to be thankful for. Most of my many, many prayers have been answered.

You couldn't have been any sweeter than you were Saturday night. What a fortunate guy I am! All the fellows say so. Bill said that your eyes were following me all night.

The sergeant told the captain that you had great big eyes.

Tell Mary that Bill had a grand time. I'd like to see her win him over. I believe it can be done. However, I'm not sure how she feels about it.

The Courtship

So Theresa is wise to us! I'll bet the others are too, but just haven't said anything about it. Neither of us can hide it, but who wants to?

From Frances, June 21, 1942, Saco, Maine

Hope you didn't run into any difficulty in getting in Saturday night. I haven't been able to get you off my mind all day.

I just finished eating a piece of mince pie. Not much sense in going to bed for a while. It's not bad enough to be kept awake thinking of you, but mince pie on top of that, I might as well sit up until morning. Mary wants to know if I'm writing my last will and testament. If she had made the mince pie, I probably would be, but seeing as Mother made it, I guess I'm safe.

I hope you get your pass to go home. Whatever you do, Gerry, don't take any chance of losing it again. I know how much my mother and father look forward to Bernard's coming home and I know your folks feel the same about you. [Bernard, my mother's brother, was in the United States Air Force.]

From Gerry, June 29, 1942, Old Orchard Beach, Maine

Gosh! But after being with you Saturday night, I've been good for nothing at all. What a tremendous let down it is to leave you and go back to soldiering.

At the beginning of this month I had thought that my cares, feelings, and affections toward you were at their height, BUT I've found out that every time I see you they soar even to much greater heights. Gee, Sweetheart! I'd never thought or dreamed it could be anything like this!

Bill says that he has a grand time whenever he sees Mary. So much so that he feels guilty because of his friendship with the other girl. I've never seen her and don't even care to. I think Mary has it all over her.

He's just about one of the best fellows I've ever met. In fact, the best! A sergeant that knows Bill and his girlfriend well, says that she isn't good enough for him.

Saturday night you wore a slight ring around your eyes. I feel I'm the cause of it. Is there anything I can do or say that'll help you get a little more sleep?

We were both tired and sleepy Saturday night but gosh, Sweetheart, it was the most wonderful sensation. I haven't got over it yet. I was too dreamy eyed all Sunday to write.

I was scanning the crowd at the parade searching for a glimpse of you, but it's just as well you didn't show up because we wouldn't have been able to talk to each other.

Here I am broke. If I had a nickel, I'd call you on the phone. It's a good thing we get free postage.

Tomorrow is supposed to be pay day, but I've heard we won't get it until Thursday. The chief trouble with this army life is that one can never make any plans or count on anything.

Gee, tomorrow is our month's anniversary. It's been the very best month of my life. We've been with each other twelve times. That's better than one out of three days. Wouldn't it be swell if the future months while we're here could be as nice.

I'm living and breathing just to be with you. I used to hate being at Saco, but now I hate being away from there. My fingers are always crossed while I'm at the factory.

If this letter has been a little too much on the romantic side, please tell me. However, every word is in total sincerity, and I always believe in facing the truth.

From Frances, June 29, 1942, Saco, Maine

I was hoping to get out to see the parade, but Mary didn't feel any too good, so I didn't suggest it. She's been so miserable with her teeth for the past three weeks that I'll be glad for her when she gets them fixed.

I had a wonderful time at the dance Saturday night, even though I was half asleep. It's a good thing they can't ration dreams.

As the summer wore on the two couples, Frances and Gerry and Mary and Bill, progressed in their relationships. There were many disappointments as the Army controlled the young soldiers' schedules and would cancel passes at the last minute leaving the girls "stood up" on frequent occasions. This was very emotionally stressful on the young lovers. The war put them on edge, but they were so grateful that it had brought them all together.

The lovebirds: Gerry and Frances, Mary and Bill

From Frances, July 6, 1942, Saco, Maine

I don't see why the time flies so when we're together and drags so when we're apart. I never realized that one person could make such a difference in everything. Whenever things go a little rough at the office, I just think of you and you'd be surprised how quickly everything else seems so unimportant.

I'm looking forward to your next night off. We keep saying, "Why did there have to be a war?" but if it weren't for it, we probably would never have the friendship that is ours.

I guess every cloud has to have a silver lining.

"Hope and pray" will have to be the watchword for us until the world and the people in it realize the stupidity of war, and take a little more time out to practice respect and love for one's neighbor.

From Gerry, July 7, 1942, Old Orchard Beach, Maine

Your last letter gave me more satisfaction than any letter I ever before received. Thanks, Sweetheart!

Gosh, but what a busy place this is. We have movies in the afternoon, movies in the early evening, and then again moonlight movies at 8:45 P.M. Not to mention dancing and music until twelve-thirty. You know, if some night you get extra lonesome, you could hop the bus at Saco and come down here for a couple of hours. I'd be able to work it out somehow. Tonight for instance, I don't go on duty until eleven-thirty.

From Gerry, July 16, 1942, Old Orchard Beach, Maine

Last night I had a chance to transfer out of the regiment, but I didn't take it. Sometimes, when I think of your crying, and missing sleep, and feeling disappointed and blue, I wonder if it would be easier for you if I did leave here. After a couple of weeks, you'd probably get back to your regular routine.

Now don't get me wrong. That's just a thought. I love you more than ever, but I don't like to see you disappointed, blue, crying, missing sleep, etc. There's never been anyone like you, and I'm always hoping someday—someday.

I'm waiting for Sunday night when I hope to see you again. But don't plan too much on it because I'm due for guard duty sometime soon.

My mind is concerned with only one thing: you, You, and YOU! Keep your spirits up. Things are always blackest before the dawn.

From Frances, July 24, 1942, Saco, Maine

It was too bad you had to be on duty last night. We left on the eleven-thirty bus. I was hoping to see you when you came off duty, but we would have been too late in getting home if we'd stayed any longer.

I don't suppose you minded walking the beach Thursday night, it was so beautiful. The moonlight glistening on the water. The night before when we were together we couldn't find the river, but last night we had a whole ocean to look at, and we couldn't be together. I guess it just proves we can't have everything.

The office manager suggested we work Sunday. I very definitely told him I would not work Sunday. There is a limit to everything and that is asking too much.

I suppose it will be Tuesday before I see you again. If it is nice Sunday we may go to the beach in the afternoon.

The Courtship

From Gerry, August 2, 1942, Old Orchard Beach, Maine

The last two days have been dry and sunny for a change. However, that doesn't make any difference to me. All I seem to want to do is lay down on my back, close my eyes, and think of you. It's a swell pastime, but it sure makes me lazy.

Wednesday night, in my estimation, was our best yet. What do you think? It sure has been nice remembering.

After getting on the train, I read your letter and then slept soundly until we reached Beverly. Then the first thing I knew, I was in the North Station.[Boston]

Everything at home was aces. My father said he would have to get a look at you and peer into the situation. My mother said that Lou, [my father's friend], said that you were a very nice girl. My father jokingly said, "You tell Lou that he isn't old enough to be a good judge".

After the first night you and Mary came here to the beach, you or Mary said you'd never come down again. But you did. Now for heaven's sake! If you ever do come down again, please! Please! Look me up! I'll try and swap shifts with one of the other fellows so that I can at least see more of you than I did those two nights.

If you are on or near the pier and see any fellow with a powder horn and leggings on, ask him to tell me that you are around. Or, if you should go to the dance hall, go right up to our look out station and tell whoever is there to get me. Now get this, I'm not encouraging you to come here. It's just in case you should get extra lonely and show up here again. The last two times I felt awfully bad about not seeing more of you. So let's not let it happen like that again.

Listen, Sweetheart! Take your full vacation and go wherever you may please. Don't let me interfere in the least way. I'll be able to go two weeks without seeing you. It'll only make it all the sweeter afterwards.

Grindstone Inn, Winter Harbor, Maine

My mother and a girlfriend from Rhode Island took their vacations together at Grindstone Inn in Winter Harbor on the Maine coast near Acadia National Park. The girls had previously waitressed together there. They both traveled by train to get there.

From Frances, August 25, 1942, Winter Harbor, Maine

I didn't mind the train trip half as much as I thought I would. Of course, you had to show up just when you did to start me off with the blues. I couldn't think straight for an hour after.

After supper Peggy and I went for a walk into the village. There aren't any streetlights at all and you should have seen us strolling along . . .Peggy had a flashlight, but we didn't use it much. We thought someone might think we were a couple of spies.

None of the guests down here have cars on account of the ration business.

Everyone said they'd take care of you for me while I was away. Are they doing as good a job as I do or better?

From Gerry, August 26, 1942, Old Orchard Beach, Maine

After seeing you for that brief hour Thursday night, I got to bed at six the next morning only to get up again at seven to go to the rifle range at Auburn. I scored second highest with the automatic rifle. We got back at seven that night. From then until darkness I cleaned the rifle. That's why you didn't get the letter I said I'd write that day. Next morning I was up early again. Back to the beloved Hotel to find a forty-eight hour pass. I called your number. Your mother said you were on your vacation and in Biddeford. [My mom worked in Biddeford, a twin city to Saco. In 1942 there were no shopping malls. The main street in Biddeford was lined with shops and small businesses.]

So the laundry not having arrived until 2:45 P.M. I waited around for it and arrived in Biddeford at 3:00 P.M. Spent an hour hoping to find you, but having no luck took the four o'clock train to Boston.

Spent Saturday night at home talking to the folks. Everyone fine. Seven o'clock Mass Sunday and then canoeing and swimming with my dad until 2:00 P.M. After a meal and some shuteye, we, the family, went to a show.

All Monday morning I was thinking of you, just hoping to see you at the train. I had made up my mind that if you were there, I was going to kiss you good-bye. BUT you offered me your hand and looked as if you were embarrassed enough as it was. Anyhow, you can't say I didn't ask you. Ever since then I've been lonely wondering how the time will pass until we are together again.

That afternoon we went to the beach to fire at a target towed by a boat. I sent six dollars worth of bullets at it. The poor tax payers.

That night I had guard duty. Was I tired and was it cold, but the moon made up for everything. What a night for your vacation to start. The weather's been perfect.

My dad's hard up for gas. When I left, he only had four gallons to last him until Sept. 22nd. So if I get twenty gallons, I'll give it to him.

What do you mean? Are they doing as good a job taking care of me as you do? Listen, Sweetheart, no one could come anywhere near doing the job you do.

The Courtship

From Gerry, August 27, 1942, Old Orchard Beach, Maine

Today's another peach. But aren't the nights cold? Last night we put on our long drawers, winter underwear. You said you liked the cold. Well, you can have it. I hate it. I'd rather roast than freeze anytime.

Well, here I am standing watch, observing ships, answering the telephone, as well as awaiting a colonel who is to inspect us. Blast him. We had to get up at seven just to get ready for him and now he hasn't even shown up yet.

Now don't tell me that there aren't any nice young gentlemen up there for you and Peggy to pass the time with.

Have you learned how to swim yet? Better hurry up because if I have to teach you, it'll be a rough tough lesson. That reminds me, I haven't seen that blue bathing suit yet. Kind of seems as though it won't be this year when I do!

Gosh, Frances, but it has been a long time. Guess I'm really starting to miss you. Well, what's a few days in a life time?

Goodnight, Sweetheart. When you're about to go to sleep, just think that there is someone keeping watch thinking of you all night.

From Frances, August 28, 1942, Winter Harbor, Maine

You mistook my emotions at the train to be from embarrassment, but the real reason was just the fact that I wanted you to kiss me but I knew if you did I'd cry.

I wasn't feeling like leaving you for two weeks. And it was bad enough not having seen you since Thursday.

There is a nice swimming pool down here and we were down there this afternoon but the water was quite cold. I was all bundled up in a sweater and jacket and I couldn't see myself even thinking of going in. There have been frosts a few nights this week.

One of the guests has a moving picture camera and machine and he showed pictures in the town hall last night.

Thanks for the candy. It was delicious.

I've got some collecting to do when I see you, but I won't need much coaxing.

From Gerry, September 1, 1942, Saco

"You Are Always in My Heart". That song was just being played on the radio. I think it is most appropriate.

Well, Sweetheart, I'll be delighted to fulfill the debt you'll be collecting when we see each other again. You'd better wear a suit of armor because I'll most likely crush you to death.

From Gerry, September 7, 1942, Quincy, Massachusetts

Gosh, Sweetheart, but it has been a long time. But it does go to show us that we can go a while without seeing each other if we ever have to.

Boy when I think it over, I am really more than fortunate in having met a sweetheart like you and being able to see you so often. Just think, we'll have a whole winter and part of the spring to look forward to. What a break! Just a lucky guy I guess.

They call me a matchmaker. Maybe I am, but it's just that I like to see any two nice people meet and enjoy each other's company.

The ration board finally gave me twelve gallons of gas after a girl went to bat for me. Some soldiers have been turned down. That really wasn't enough for me to go up to see you and take you around a bit. So I just stayed at home.

Saturday and Sunday afternoons I spent on my bicycle. It was swell but I'm not in trim for it. My knees were a little weak. Guess I'm really getting old. If this war doesn't hurry up and get over I'll be good for nothing.

I'm expecting to arrive at the Biddeford station at 9:37 P.M. Thursday night. So if you should be around town at that time, well it would be nice seeing you. If not, I'll call the house and if you're at home, I'll be up because I'll have an hour or so before eleven o'clock.

Well the radio is playing "The Very Thought of You". I never did enjoy love songs as much as I do now that you give them a meaning.

It's roast turkey and blueberry pie for supper. Boy oh boy! Eating is my pet vice. Guess you'll have to be the one to make me curb it.

From Frances, September 8, 1942, Saco, Maine

I'm having an awful time trying to write this letter. Mary and Theresa are pestering me. When I opened your letter tonight, Mary got a glimpse of the salutation and she naturally told Theresa. They've been riding me ever since. We got a letter from Bernard today and Mary said if I wanted to read his letter, she'd have to see mine. Don't you think she needs another spanking?

I certainly appreciated your letter. Maybe some day I'll acquire the knack of expressing my thoughts as well as you do.

The work wasn't too bad today. Although things could be better, I just didn't let it bother me. Everyone was glad to see me back and told me so. I guess that's why I feel so good.

I'll try and meet you Thursday night, but if I shouldn't, call up the house.

From Gerry, September 13, 1942, Old Orchard Beach, Maine

Gee, but it was swell of you to have come to the train last Thursday. If you hadn't, I don't believe I'd have seen much of you. As it was, it was little enough, but not enough. All the way up on the train I was planning to kiss you as soon as I saw you. In fact, I thought that those two hours and thirty-seven minutes would never go by. But when I did arrive, and had to walk the length of about three cars, and face Bill and Mary. Oh well, I just didn't think you'd have liked it so well. So after bumping into Bill first, it wouldn't have been right to have kissed you after having shaken hands with him. But there'll come a day. I'll make it up to you.

When I did get back to the factory, I found out that I could have just as well have stayed out until at least twelve-thirty. Boy, did that burn me up, and then on top of that, we had to come out here the next morning.

From Gerry, September 21, 1942, Old Orchard Beach, Maine

This morning I am acting as corporal. Just sitting down, answering the telephone, listening to the radio, and enjoying the luxury of an electric heater and light. What a snap! One would hardly believe that a war was existing.

Gosh, Frances, but you sure made me happy Friday night. My mind has been continuously thinking of you and us ever since. The more I think of the situation, the more I am resolved that prayer is the only solution. I can't help but believe that everything will turn out for the best, and that we'll be very happy. If anyone deserves to be so, it certainly is you and that is what I want mostly.

Just think. Wednesday is practically here. It seems as though I am only living to see you. Nothing else seems to bother me.

41

We now have a little more liberty. They've decided to let us out on the nights we have fire guard duty. So things look pretty good for Wednesday. I'd like to take you places and do things, but there's a catch. Pay day came around while I was on furlough. So I didn't get paid this month. However, next month will soon be here.

It's raining hard. The wind is cold and blowing strongly. I feel like a heel sitting here while the other privates are suffering on the beach.

The radio just started playing "Just a Kiss in the Dark". My heart sunk. Loneliness filled it. Now it's "What is This Thing Called Love". It's the greatest thing in the world.

Well, Sweetheart, keep your faith, hope, and chin up and your eyes dry. I'll not let you down. You should be sleeping now. I'd like to see you asleep.

From Frances, September 23, 1942, Saco, Maine

You certainly made me feel blue tonight when you said you were still down at the beach. Lately, every time I plan on seeing you, something turns up.

I'm sending you one of the pictures I had taken when I was on my vacation. I was relaxing in a beach chair when Peggy decided to take my picture. I said, "Go ahead".

Do you think it looks like me, or have you forgotten what I look like? I'll show you the others when, and if, I see you. I don't believe in being definite any more.

You should have seen me tonight when you called. The operator spoke first. I knew right away you were still at the beach, but I wouldn't believe it until you told me. I was hoping and praying that I was mistaken, but I wasn't.

It's a good thing we were eating supper. I had my back to the dining room so they couldn't see the tears, but I guess they knew they were there. I just started crying again, so I guess I'll "hit the hay", and see if I can sleep it off.

From Gerry, September 24, 1942, 4:45 A.M., Old Orchard Beach

If ever there was anything I hated doing, it was calling you last night and telling you that I couldn't see you. It really bothered me so much so that I couldn't doze off to sleep. I was extra tired, but thinking of what a shame it was to have to disappoint you again, kept my mind too much ill at ease for the sandman to do his stuff.

Here I've been sitting up since eleven forty-five just feeling blue. It all happened just because of a slug nosed sergeant who decided not to come out this trip. But at nine o'clock he showed up, just so that he could have a date. He asked me if I wanted to stay out here four more days. I said, "NO!"

Then he said that I'd be going back tomorrow noon, but now he's decided to go himself. So I'm stuck. When

I'll see you again, I don't know, but I do know one thing, and that is that it can't be too soon to suit me.

However, I do believe that all these disappointments just help to make our love all the stronger.

What do you think?

I'm rapidly approaching the state in which it would be practically impossible to go on living without lovely you.

What a moon this week, and to think that we can't share it in each other's glorious company.

Well, Sweetheart, always remember, that no matter what happens, you are tops with me, and I'll never let you down.

All my friends are always asking as to how you are. They all think you are swell.

From Gerry, September 24, 1942, 8:20 P.M., Old Orchard Beach, Maine

Just think. This is the second letter on the same day. That's a record so far. Imagine, I slept from six this morning until four this afternoon. Then, after eating and washing up, what could have been nicer than that letter from you. I felt kind of guilty because I was just mailing yours at the time.

So, Sweetheart, you should get one Friday and another Saturday. I'll be anxiously awaiting your next. We even get mail on Sundays. (Hint.)

Thanks for the snapshot. What do you mean? Have I forgotten what you look like? That day will never come. How could I possibly forget such a face which means so much to me? No! No more of that sort of stuff from you!

Gee, Sweetheart, I wish you wouldn't cry so often, or at least wait until I'm with you to dry them away.

Right now I can't even give you an idea as to when I'll see you again. If they had their way, I'd be out here all the time. They wanted to keep me out here for sixteen days, but I squawked.

Don't be blue, Frances. We'll be together again. Probably before you'll expect. Anyhow, we know we both love each other, so what else matters.

From Gerry, Saturday, September 26, 2:06 A.M., Old Orchard Beach, Maine

The last day has been a most uneasy one for me. Always on my mind was the thought of how much I want to see you, and how soon or long it will be before I can. Never before has anything bothered me as much as that has. I'm hoping and praying that it'll be Sunday. That would be before you would get this.

What did I ever do to deserve such a perfect sweetheart as you are? Gosh, sometimes I wonder if it's real.

That out of sight, out of mind stuff is the bull! I'll vouch for "Absence makes the heart grow fonder".

Three more days and we will have known each other four whole months. Golly, but it seems so much longer than that. It makes me kind of wonder what the next four months will bring. Peace seems so far off. Everything's so uncertain. Guess living for each day is the most advisable policy. Do you think you can do that?

I hold Saint Francis responsible for our meeting. My thanks to him never can be great enough. I can't help but believe he'll see us through. It was as I had hoped— love at first sight. Some thrill and experience! Eh?

You are all I'd hoped for, all I'd dreamed about, and all I'd prayed for. In fact, a lot, lot more. Thanks for everything, Fran, dear. I'll try my very best to be worthy of you.

From Gerry, September 26, 1942, Old Orchard Beach, Maine

I've lost six pounds this past week. If we want any sleep, it means sacrificing a few meals. Can you imagine my getting by on just one meal a day? Well, I have on three different days. Nothing seems important any more except being with you.

Gee! To think that in only twenty-one hours , I should be climbing your front steps, and you will be standing in the door waiting for me.

Here's predicting that my next "goodnight'" will be in the manner you like best.

The Courtship

From Frances, October 1, 1942, Saco, Maine

How do you feel after your pass? Did you sleep on the train? It didn't take me very long to fall asleep after you left. How were all your folks at home?

I was looking for you this morning, but I didn't see you. I thought you might walk down by the office before going back to the "hotel". [The "hotel" was a slang reference to the shoe factory in Saco.] *Anne caught me looking out the window more than once.*

You have certainly been on my mind since the other night. I told you before that it didn't interfere with my work, but I can't say that now.

I'm so tired now that I don't feel like writing. I just want to close my eyes and think of you. I think I'd better go to bed before I fall asleep on the table.

From Gerry, October 2, 1942, 4:25 A.M., Old Orchard Beach, Maine

Gee! But it was swell to have seen so much of you last week. I was well contented and more or less figured that we had made up for not having seen more of each other for so long. My only regret was that I was broke and so couldn't have taken you to a show, or bowling, or for a snack somewhere. However, we enjoyed each other's company and that's what counts most.

The train was late, but I'd have easily made it anyhow. I had exactly twenty-four hours with my folks.

When I arrived, my father jokingly asked what I was doing coming in at such an hour and said, "So you had a date."

My mother said, "That's his privilege."

I told her that we had it bad and showed them those two snaps you gave me. She said something about making sure and the topic was dropped.

Last night I was invited to a party. Lou and Frank and the sergeant and some of the other fellows went. But I didn't go in spite of their pleading. I wouldn't have been able to enjoy myself anyhow, mostly because there would be other girls there, and without you I'd be bored.

As a matter of fact, I've reached a new state of affairs. I'm deeply concerned about us. I don't believe I'll ever be contented until that plain round metallic emblem of union presents itself in the proper place. Feeling that way, I can appreciate how you must feel. If only circumstances were different. That problem is always on my mind. Now more than ever. Every day it gets worse. It makes me wonder when a climax will be reached and then what? Anyhow I believe everything will happen for the best, and that we'll get to our goal and have nothing to regret.

My name was put in for corporal, but I doubt very much if I will get it because I say whatever I think and I don't pour the gravy over people I don't like.

Well, Sweetheart, I've sent you some candy.

Keep courage and we'll get there some day.

From Gerry, October 2, 1942, 8:45 P.M., Old Orchard Beach, Maine

I just this minute said goodnight to you. Your voice sounded swell. I'd like to listen to you all night, but even over the phone, we lack privacy.

For the first time I'll have to admit that I'm stuck for words. All I know is that I want to be with you. The sooner the better, the more often the better.

If this war doesn't show signs of ending fairly soon, I think I'll dwindle away to a shadow. Guess it's best not to even think of such things.

Well, Sweetheart, once again it's a written goodnight, but soon I hope it'll be a verbal one accompanied by an overwhelming embrace.

From Gerry Sunday, October 4, 1942, 6:15 A.M., Old Orchard Beach, Maine

When I called last night, I was kind of hoping that you'd be able to come here and go to the show with me. But I'm glad you didn't because I'd have been much concerned about you getting home safely and without a scary feeling.

After phoning you, I went to confession and then to the movies. "Bullet Scars" and "Always in My Heart" were playing. I enjoyed the last film mostly because I like the song so well.

Funny thing, I was in church ahead of time. The priest entered and, seeing me saying the Rosary, asked

if I were praying for my wife. I said that I wasn't married.
But it would have been the same if I were, because I was
praying for you.

While I've been writing this, another day has
been dawning. To me it means another nearer you
and our goal. I wonder how much faith, hope, and
patience I possess.

Here I am out of words again, but in another
hour I'll be at Mass and then I'll find words for you,
Sweetheart.

From Gerry, October 4, 1942, 8:50 P.M., Old Orchard Beach, Maine

The news just crept out. I'm stuck again for another
four days. But, anyhow, that should give me a good part
of the coming week-end to spend with lovely you.

What'll we do? I mean perhaps you would have
some ideas, desires, suggestions, preferences. Not that
it makes any difference to me. Just your being there or
rather with me is all that's necessary for my happiness.

I just finished rolling cigarettes for the boys. It was
some temptation to try one myself, but I thought
twice and saved myself the grief.

So you think that you are going to get out of teach-
ing Sunday school. Oh! No! It's not going to be as easy
as you think it will. Father Mac will have you right
back on the job, or I miss my guess.

The Courtship

From Frances, October 4, 1942, Saco, Maine

You should have seen me at the dance last night. I went on three of those whirling affairs. There were two soldiers pretty well lit who insisted on getting into the dance. They didn't have any partners. They came near getting into a fight with the cop who was trying to get them to sit down. He called the sergeant over. He turned to the sidelines and asked for two of us to go on the dance floor and settle the argument. Mary wouldn't go because she gets dizzy, but Santa and I went and the dance went off ok.

About an hour later three M.P.s came in and talked to the sergeant. They picked out three soldiers and took them outside. They weren't seen again the rest of the evening.

My cousin Joe, visiting from Lawrence, Massachusetts, had a wonderful time at the dance. I hope you get back in time to meet him. I danced quite a bit with him. I could never remember his name. All I could think of was you. I'd go to say something and call him "Gerry." He says I've got it bad! [My maternal grandparents had gone by train to New Brunswick, Canada to visit an ailing relative.]

From Frances, October 7, 1942, Saco, Maine

It certainly is wonderful to have my folks home. I had to laugh the other night when you asked if I gave them a big kiss when they got home.

Mary and I met my father down on Maple Street when we were going to work. He was coming home after the car to go back and pick up my mother at the train station. We both gave him a kiss right then and there. I don't know what anyone would think to see that so early in the morning.

I've been disappointed so many times by planning on seeing you and having something turn up so I couldn't that I don't dare to think about Friday—never mind making any plans. I haven't had a good cry for quite a while, but I won't guarantee anything if I don't see you Friday.

You should have been up here last night. Margaret and Hartley, [an older brother of my mom's and his wife], *were up. They were kidding me about you. Of course, Mary had to tell them I got two letters yesterday. They said we must have it bad. They don't know the half of it.*

From Gerry, October 7, 1942, Old Orchard Beach, Maine

To think that it'll only be two more nights and then—Woo! Woo! Gosh, but I can hardly wait. I don't care what they say, eight days is too much. To see you again. Seems as if that's all I'm living for. I can't help but think, dream, and hope for that big, big day!

You sounded swell tonight. I wonder why you were so jovial, especially after answering three false alarms.

It's got so that I don't feel right unless I call you every night. How do you feel about it?

I don't know why it should be, but lately I find it awfully hard to think of something to write. Even over the telephone I'm stuck for words or even topics. Possibly it's because I've become more or less one track minded. There's been one big thought on my mind lately. I'm always wrestling with it. When and how, why and why not. Gee, Sweetheart, you've got me in an awful state of affairs. What am I going to do about it? Normally there's two solutions to such a situation. Either sever relations entirely or take the fatal step. Now with the first remedy out of the question, the second becomes the entangling force of convictions. So I'm resolved that all we can do is pray, pray, and pray. Harder and more earnestly than ever. How good a job can we do? With the whole winter in front of us, we've got something to work on. I wish you'd talk more about the predicament. I'm going to need a lot of help.

From Frances, October 12, 1942

You must have thought I was a little 'tetched' tonight when you called. Father Gosselin was here. He is Father Mac's assistant. When the phone rang, I was sitting by the radio and, of course, I answered it.

Right off the priest said, "Aha, her boyfriend."

Of course they all got a kick out of the fact he guessed right.

He said, "It's too bad we're all here. Tell him Monday night is a bad night to call."

It's the first time we had met him, but he has been here all summer. He's helping Father Mac take the fall census.

We were all set to tell Father Mac that we couldn't teach Sunday school, but he didn't come. We're no further ahead than we ever were.

From Gerry, October 18, 1942, 6:10 P.M., Old Orchard Beach, Maine

Here am I, quite comfortable, sitting upstairs in the firehouse, writing at a table for a change. Was I lucky this morning. I was sleeping at the company command post instead of on the pier, and I woke up just ten minutes before the last Mass was to start. If I ever missed Mass, I'd be feeling miserable, but thanks to some hidden power I didn't.

I'll be here at the firehouse writing letters until they kick me out at ten o'clock. Not counting your letters, I have twelve letters to answer. Some date as far back as June. Isn't that terrible? Ever since I met you, all of my friends and acquaintances take a back seat. My biggest, greatest, most devout attentions concern you, Sweetheart.

I'll bet that you taught Sunday school again today, and that you'll still be doing so when Christmas arrives. Then after teaching so long, you'll have to finish the year. The only way you'll ever get out of it is to get married and move away.

Gee, it was swell seeing you those five out of eight nights I spent in Saco. Here's looking forward to Wednesday night because then I hope to be with you again, Sweetheart.

I like your eight little nephews and nieces. You're lucky. Look at me. I'm not even an uncle yet. But just think, all I'd have to do, is marry you and I'd be their uncle.

It was a good thing that you explained why you were laughing so much that night I phoned while Father Gosselin was there. I didn't know what to think.

It's a good thing they send me out to the beach, or I'd be walking up your steps every night and that wouldn't be right. I wanted in the worst way to see you last Thursday and Friday nights, but it was probably better that I didn't because you needed the rest. Then again, it is only right and proper that you have a few nights to yourself.

Well, Sweetheart, we've got one consolation. Every day is another day towards the day. [He is referring to their future wedding day.] Not only that, but the fifteenth of the month is here and gone, and I'm still here. I've been thinking that if we go on as we have been doing, and I'm here for the duration, I probably will regret not having taken that big step before Armistice. However, as I've said before, I'm leaving it in God's hands, and praying that the Blessed Virgin and the Saints will intercede for us.

Guess I've said enough for one letter. Keep your spirits up, Sweetheart. Everything turns out for the best. We've no regrets so far, and I don't believe we will. I'll be seeing you soon, and until then, just stay as sweet as you are.

From Frances, October 20, 1942, Saco, Maine

It was wonderful to hear your voice last night on the phone. I was hoping to get a letter Saturday because I thought you had gone to the beach. I was home all alone after you called because everyone had gone out.

Do you still have to sleep out there on the pier? You must have plenty of bedding, or else you'd freeze. I don't think you would enjoy that.

How is your mouth? Does it bother you very much? Next time, sample your soup before guzzling it down!

From Gerry, October 20, 1942, 7:25 P.M., Old Orchard Beach, Maine

Another night has gone by, and again I missed out on telephoning you. I've been busy here in our kitchen up over the firehouse. Our cook was transferred to the parachute troops just this afternoon. So, it being my turn for K.P. today, I was also selected to prepare the evening meal. Made out OK. But it would never do for me to take over the job as cook, because I'd never be able to stop eating and then, oh well! I don't even need to mention the consequences.

The job was already offered to me a couple of times. It would mean staying out here all the time, no walking on the beach, and only cooking for sixteen men from seven in the morning until six. Then I'd have every night off to come and go as I please, but transportation isn't so hot, and I wouldn't like being cooped up in this stuffy place all day.

Guess I won't be sleeping on the pier any more. Suits me. It would cost the owners an extra fifty dollars a thousand for fire insurance if we had any kind of a stove out there. So, no heat and plenty of cold and damp bedding.

Well, Sweetheart, it's back on the beach at ten-thirty, and I'm already dead tired. So I'll be thinking of you before getting what little sleep I can before then. And then, all through my patrolling, it'll be you, You, and YOU foremost in my mind.

Our complete happiness will depend upon how hard we pray, so let's not spare the 'orses, Sweetheart. We'll get there and probably sooner than we'll expect.

From Frances, October 26, 1942, Saco, Maine

This is only the second attempt at a letter to you tonight. I threw the other away. Things didn't go any *too smoothly in the office today and it sort of got the best of me.*

I hope you weren't late in getting back last night.

Honestly, Gerry, I've never had such a hard time to write a letter as I'm having tonight. I'm in a daze, I guess. All I can think of is you, and the minute I start to write anything it doesn't make sense.

I've got a newspaper here by me all covered with scratches. If you could read Chinese or hieroglyphics, maybe you'd guess what I've been thinking. As it is, my thoughts are so jumbled tonight, that every time I concentrate on one thing, I get so sidetracked, I'm at the point of quitting.

From Gerry, October 29, 1942, Old Orchard Beach, Maine

Surely by now you are wondering just why you haven't heard from me. Have I forgotten you? What's the matter with me? When are you going to see me again, etc., etc.?

Well, Sweetheart, I've been on the go all the time. When it's time to call you, I'm either on the beach or slaving away in the kitchen cleaning after eighteen grub thirsty men.

Thanks for not going to the formal. After all I must admit I would be somewhat jealous. But of course understand you are always free to come and go as you please. As ever, you are still without chains! But some day your apron strings will be well weighted down.

So you were in a tough fix trying to write that last letter. What's the real reason? I mean the particular thoughts that were so heavily preying on your mind?

I can't read Chinese and I know nothing about hieroglyphics, so you'll have to give me the low down.

Well, because of a parade yesterday, it'll be Saturday before we get back to Saco. So keep the flame burning for me and I'll be there to enjoy its warmth.

From Frances, November 4, 1942, Saco, Maine

Ann, [a friend of my mother], *was asking for you today. She wanted to know if you were still playing cupid. I wish someone else would play cupid and aim at you. Maybe it would get results?*

I think I'd better go to bed. There are a million thoughts running around in my head, but I can't seem to get them down on paper. I try to make sense to them and I find myself falling asleep. They all simmer down to you and I. Maybe some day I can straighten them out and tell you everything.

We've got to rely on our faith and prayers to pull us through this war and into a decent peace. Sometimes it seems pretty dark, but it's always darkest before the dawn.

Do you think I'll see you before you get your next forty-eight? Four days without seeing you is too much. Don't you think so?

From Gerry, November 6, 1942, 3:58 A.M., Old Orchard Beach, Maine

Here's guessing that you've just breathed, "It's about time". It was sure swell of you to have written to me after having worked late and bowled. You really have got it bad. Your mind was well into a muddled state of affairs. Now you've got me waiting for the day that you are going to straighten out your thoughts and tell me everything.

Just what did you mean when you said, "I wish someone else would play cupid and aim at you. Maybe it would get results?"

I demand an explanation. Just what results do you want?

Well I'm back on the snap job again. Acting corporal, answering the phone etc. Only catch is that we now have our meals delivered already cooked and we're not eating half so well. However, that shouldn't do me any harm.

Right now it's before dawn and is it dark! Wow! Our paralleled situation keeps preying on my mind. In spite of all the uncertainty, I strongly feel that we'll know the final solution by this time next year. Is that encouraging or discouraging?

Don't think I'll see you again until Tuesday or Wednesday. However, it can't be too soon and one never knows when , so keep your spirits up, and just think how lucky we are to still be together.

The Courtship

From Gerry, November 8, 1942, 4:15 A.M., Old Orchard Beach, Maine

Little did I know that while I was talking to you last night, the second front was being opened up. Do you know what that means to you and me?

We now have a ray of light. The war in Europe should be over before 1944. I might be shipped out any time, so it is best that we wait until the war is over before we make any plans and marry. To me, I'm partly relieved. Things are happening. The future looks a little brighter.

Tonight I went to confession. While saying my penance, the priest asked me to remain. We chatted until after ten o'clock. Got real chummy. I told him about you. He said it is better not to get married while the war is going on. So, Sweetheart, it looks as though we should wait. It'll help make marriage more worthwhile, give our love the real test, and anything that's worthwhile is worth waiting for. As I've said before, I won't let you down, Frances. Trust in me. I'm trusting in you.

Remember , every hour is an hour nearer our goal. Every step I take will be another step nearer life together.

Fourteen of our non-comms are being transferred to help make the nucleus of two new divisions. So it looks as though I'll be a corporal soon, or also be transferred.

The most important thing I have to say is never stop praying, Sweetheart. I love you.

From Frances, November 12, 1942, Saco, Maine

I hope you didn't worry about me after last night. I suppose I should be able to control my emotions better than that, but when I start crying I just can't stop. Generally when I feel one of those spells coming on, I get off by myself. But last night was once when I couldn't.

You started me [crying] when you said if we could plan on our being married a year from this coming spring.

When I said my thoughts were practically the same as yours, you saw the loop hole in practically.

I couldn't say they were exactly the same as yours because I hadn't thought of it in regard to years or even months or days. I always pray that it would be as soon as possible.

I've never tried to look ahead too far because I've found that when I do, something generally happens, and all my plans are in vain. Although I agree with you that we should wait until the war is over before making any definite plans.

I hope you don't have to stay down there eight days because I would like to see you sooner than that.

From Gerry, November 20, 1942, Pine Point, a few miles up the coast from Old Orchard Beach, Maine

Back here again. This time I'm told that it's for four days again, but I can't help but think that I'll be out on duty for eight days. However, if I am, and at the end of those eight days I have another forty-eight hour pass, I'll be tickled because it would fall on a week-end , and I'd be hoping to take you home with me. My dad said that would be swell. My mother said to bring you home on that Saturday. My mother said to do so and that you could stay overnight. Gee, Sweetheart, that would be swell. What do you think?

Well at last I finally received your letter. It wasn't mailed until the eighteenth. That girl must have carried it around with her for a whole week. I was really worried about it. I figured that if I didn't get that letter, I'd never find out how your thoughts differ from mine. After reading that letter, I'm much relieved because after all your ideas aren't any different from mine.

Well, Sweetheart, as things are averaging out, I do get to see you on the average of two nights a week. That's not too bad, is it? In fact, if I were a civilian, I'd more than likely not be able to see you that much.

From Frances, November 23, 1942, Saco, Maine

I was certainly pleased to get your letter this evening. I worked until quarter of seven and then walked home. I feel so tired. It's just as well you're at the outpost tonight. My back aches and I feel tired everywhere. We have to get the payroll out a day earlier this week and I worked ten hours today. I didn't have any supper until I got home.

Tonight when I was walking home, I met Bill Pease and Mary on their way to the show.

Gee! It's terrible walking alone after dark. I'm so used to having you toss me over the rough places, that I stumble all the time.

It would be wonderful if you did get another forty-eight hour pass on a week-end. I'm looking forward to meeting your folks.

When I told Mary and my mother that you might be kept out eight days, Mother said, "I guess we'll have to be giving you a forty-eight hour pass"!

I don't know if I act that bad, or if they're only kidding.

From Gerry, November 26, 1942, Break Water Farm, Maine

Today is a real Thanksgiving day for me. Even though I am in the Army and away from home and especially you, I still have many, many things for which to be thankful.

Here I am sitting on the end of my cot, writing on an old plant table, burning an old kerosene lantern, and thinking very heavily of you. Ever since I came to this secluded man's land, I've been thinking of you. That's all I want to do.

Lou, [my father's friend], *and I share a pleasant upstairs room in this old abandoned farm homestead. Especially while I'm in this room, I think of you and us. Never so much before as now. I'm in a terrible muddled state. There will be only one remedy for my condition and that is you. The DAY,* [He is again referring to their future wedding day.], *seems so evident and still so indefinite. It can't come too soon to suit me. But still, I want to be able to say, "Here's our home. You take possession of it and I'll be home to you every night".*

Gosh, Sweetheart, I hardly am able to write. Lonesome for you, that's the whole story. Our not being able to have this week-end together has greatly disappointed me. My hopes to be with you and have you meet the folks and vice versa are so high that every passing week-end without a pass is a blow to me.

Well, Sweetheart, it's time for me to get ready to walk the coastline. I've been bent over this paper and haven't said hardly anything for this last hour. Guess the only way is for us to be together. Then I can pour out every last thought. I should have written a longer letter, but I want you to get this tomorrow or Saturday at the latest.

From Frances, November 26, 1942, Saco, Maine

It was swell of you to call me today. It's been so long since we've had any time together. I was more or less expecting to meet your folks this week-end. Then your friend Hunt called and said you'd be out until Sunday.

Lately I can't do anything unless I associate it with you somehow or other. What do you recommend?

From Frances, December 15, 1942, Saco, Maine

How is everything in the dear old Army? Although it's only been two days since I've seen you, it seems ages.

I'm really looking forward to meeting your folks this week-end, and I'm going to be quite disappointed if I don't.

It doesn't seem to matter how much I see you lately. It seems as if I spend most of my time wondering when we'll be together again.

All day I've been thinking of writing this letter and now that I've actually started, I can't think of a thing to write. I started out by writing out my Christmas cards, and I didn't even get one written. I couldn't keep my mind on it. I looked at about a dozen cards and put them away.

When I write one sentence, I sort of dream for about fifteen minutes, and I'm practically asleep before I get ambition enough to write more.

From Gerry, December 15, 1942, Higgins Beach, near Cape Elizabeth and Portland, Maine

Just arrived here at Will Pease's old haunt. Last night I cornered the top kick and asked him if I could go on outpost today and have a forty-eight hour pass when I go in Saturday. After thinking awhile, he said yes. He was in a good mood, having just returned from a week-end pass himself.

What a break, Sweetheart, just the one I've been awaiting for the last few months. Here's hoping that everything will turn out OK, and that you'll be going home with me.

The chances are that I'll not get to Saco until about two-thirty Saturday. So the four o'clock train out of Biddeford would be the one that we'd likely take. That would get us at my house about three and one half hours later. That wouldn't be too bad, would it? Then coming back we could take a train from Boston at 7:00 P.M. Sunday, or 2:20 A.M. Monday morning whichever would be better for you.

I can't help but think how swell it would be traveling with you, and especially having the folks meet you.

Gosh! I've been on the go ever since I left you Sunday. Rushing all the time to get the bikes finished so that I'd be ready to get out here this afternoon and thus more or less insure having a pass Saturday.

From Gerry, December 17, 1942, Higgins Beach, Maine

This morning it was ten below zero for a few hours. Rather snappy out. Cold enough for you?

Today they relieved the boys who are going on pass at 10:30 so that they could catch the twelve o'clock train for Boston. It looks as though they might make a steady thing of this practice. So I am writing you to let you know that I might be ready to catch that twelve o'clock train Saturday. I wouldn't want to notify you the last minute. Anyhow, it should be either the twelve or four o'clock train and even at that, I can't promise that I'll have time to meet you at your house. You might possibly have to go the station without my being your escort. However, I'll be sure to telephone you.

Don't go to any bother about anything. Just come as you are. You're always good enough for me. So I'm in the same boat that you travel in. I've many letters to write, and Christmas cards to address. But just can't seem to get down to it, and put my mind on it.

Well, Sweetheart, keep your fingers crossed. It's about time that we got this break.

From Gerry, December 29, 1942, Old Orchard Beach, Maine

Already last Sunday night seems to be so far away, and next Sunday night even so much further away. Anyhow, Sweetheart, we were very fortunate in having had Saturday and Sunday evenings with each other.

Because of your tears, I couldn't help but think that you were terribly disappointed in not having received a diamond for Christmas. However, I do know that there was much more to it than that. Gosh, but I wish that you could be comfortable and still pour out your heart and thoughts to me.

Thanks for having gone to Mass Saturday morning. It was swell of you. Every time you do go to church I can't help but believe that it does help and will help our situation and future.

That ring you so thoughtfully gave to me is really flashy. It constantly reminds me of you. Today I really christened it. Some how or other, I put a couple of teeny scratches in it. I've always been tough on material things. Just a proverbial "Bull in a China Closet". See what you are letting yourself in for.

I'm still inclined to believe that forty-four will be our big year. Even that wouldn't be too tough. You'd still be a young bride. Besides, I still have to prove myself worthy of you.

A soldier and the love of his life.

From Frances, December 29, 1942, Saco, Maine

I hope you haven't been worrying about me too much. Just think, I haven't cried since last night. After you called up, I was feeling sort of blue. I guess Mary understood although she didn't say anything about it. She just casually suggested a show. So we went and saw Abbott and Costello [movie] and another show.

It was sleeting out tonight when we came home. It must be pretty miserable to have to be out in it for any length of time. I hope you won't have to get out in it too often. Or don't you mind it?

I wish this war were over so people could get back to a normal way of living. There are plenty of others in the same boat as us, and they are all looking forward to the peace which will follow. It is my fervent prayer that we won't have to wait too long and that the peace which follows will have been worth the cost. The future is something that only God knows, and we must rely on his mercy.

CHAPTER THREE

1943–An Eventful Year

From Frances, January 6, 1943, Saco, Maine

I don't want you to think I'm selfish because it isn't that. It's because I love you so much and the uncertainty of everything gets me down. But there's one thing that keeps my spirits up. It's our love.

From Gerry, January 8, 1943,
Old Orchard Beach, Maine

All during my forty-eight hour leave I was good for nothing but thinking of you. What a state. I was around the house most of the time just sitting droopily and moping. Never before had I missed you so much. What am I coming to? What are we going to do?

Congrats on being considered for supervisor. You've got the stuff. Be sure and accept it if you are approached again. Besides you're going to need experience supervising so that you'll be able to supervise me, our brood, and household. Ha! Ha! Ha!

From Frances, January 14, 1943, Saco Maine

Just had a blackout for twenty minutes. There was one place up on North Street that had a light showing all the time.

I'm really praying that by this coming summer events will have taken a turn for the better and we will be able to make a few plans.

Right now I think the wisest thing to do is pray, pray, and pray, so that we will keep our love pure and worthy of the favors we are asking.

During this time period, my parents came to a decision to take the big step and get married as the following letter passages confirm.

From Gerry, January 22, 1943, Old Orchard Beach, Maine

It sure was nice being able to be with you those four nights in a row. But every night only gets me in the mood never to leave you.

Well. Sweetheart, no matter what happens or how long the days seem, every second will be a second nearer our great start together. In many ways, I'm glad that Lent is coming along. It'll really give us a chance to prepare as any worthy couple should.

Never be timid about expressing any of your thoughts or ideas, because, after all, you are the one who'll be sacrificing the most. Do you fully realize that you'll have to be ready for any eventuality? Gee,

Sweetheart! It's asking an awful lot of you. In fact, sometimes I wonder if it isn't too much to ask of any girl in such conditions as these. However, if it is what you want most, then so it is with me, and so it will be. We'll have to take the risks and chances. I've always taken chances and would rather now than never.

Sweetheart, every breath I take is for you. No matter what might happen, I'll endure everything for you. It's got to be, and it will be.

From Frances, January 22, 1943, Saco, Maine

You should see how they have dimmed the street lights. They only show a small circle of light around each post. They might just as well put them out entirely.

I guess I'll have to work all day tomorrow on the Social Security Report. ... We are given thirty days to get it out and it is generally left until the last minute. Then someone has to take it to Boston. With gas being rationed now, they'll have to make it coincide with the train schedule whether they like it or not.

From Gerry, January 29, , 1943, Old Orchard Beach, Maine

Gee, Sweetheart, I can't wait to see Father Mac. Everything is hanging in mid air now, but then we'll be all set. I hope! I hope! I hope!

Today the Captain said, "The lover he was known as in those days."

I said, "What do you mean those days?"

He said, "When are you going to be married?"
I said, "Next March, I hope."
He said, "What year?"
I said, "'43."
He said, "Did you write and tell your mother about
this girl?"
I said, "Yes."
"Did you take her home with you?"
"Yes."
So that was that!
Last night I told Bill that we'd like Mary and him
to stand up for us. He was very pleased.

On February 5, 1943, my mother's brother Jack died unexpectedly at age thirty-six leaving four small children and a wife. My dad was with my mom at the family home when she received the news. The two of them along with my Aunt Mary walked to Main Street where Jack and his family lived. They stayed with the children until their mother arrived home from work. My father led the praying of the Rosary as they walked to Jack's apartment.

Sometime in February the official engagement occurred and my dad gave my mom her diamond. It may possibly and most likely have taken place on Valentine's Day.

On March 6, 1943 my mom and dad were married at Most Holy Trinity Catholic Church in Saco, Maine. The reception was held at the home of my grandparents. My dad played the violin and some of his soldier friends played other instruments. A great time was had by all!

Gerard Edward Cameron and Frances Barbara Colpitts,
married March 6, 1943 in Saco, Maine.

My mom and dad then boarded a train in Biddeford and headed to New York City where they honeymooned at the Brown Hotel and enjoyed sites and experiences in the Big Apple.

Many years later my mom and I stayed at the same hotel when I went for my interview at the College of New Rochelle from which I received my B.A. in 1966.

In the spring of 1943 my dad was promoted to corporal. By May, my mom was not feeling well. My dad was encouraging her to go to the doctor. You guessed it. She was pregnant with me.

Before the war, my dad had his own bicycle shop. He brought a tandem to Maine. My Aunt Theresa told me that he and my pregnant mom extensively pedaled that bicycle built for two over the country roads surrounding Saco whenever possible during that summer of '43. Even my maternal grandfather tried it out!

Because of the uncertainties and unpredictable circumstances of the times, my parents did not set up housekeeping. My mom remained at home with her parents while my dad came and went whenever possible according to his military schedule.

My dad's people loved the water and the beach. My dad enjoyed swimming in the stimulating cold Maine ocean waters during those warm summer months. His enjoyment of the ocean was clearly expressed in these written words to my mom.

After I called you last night, I had a rollicking, frolicking time wallowing around in the water. I was just like a big walrus. The water was so grand that if I hadn't had to get some sleep I'd have been tempted to stay all night.

My father's matchmaking came to fruition when my mom's older sister Mary married my father's buddy Bill Pease. Of him my dad wrote on June 30, 1943:

Last night Bill and I sat up until three o'clock telling each other about how fortunate we are to have you and Mary and your folks for in-laws.

He's the finest fellow I know. Mary will never be sorry. He really loves her dearly. It is by no means a marriage of convenience or anything like that! He'll go more than halfway. I hope that everything will turn out as nicely for them as it has for us. He's just about as pure and innocent as any man could be. The four of us should have much happiness and many good times together.

On July 17, my Aunt Mary and Uncle Bill tied the knot. They were married in the same church as my parents and had their reception at my grandparents' home where all were again entertained by soldier musicians. They left by train for their honeymoon in the White Mountains of New Hampshire.

Like my parents, they delayed setting up housekeeping because of the war. Thus my grandparents had two married daughters at home with soldier husbands who came and went as their military schedules allowed.

A few weeks after Mary Colpitts married Bill Pease, my dad commented on the "lovey-dovey" Peases giving each other shampoos to pass the time. He was grateful to them for taking my mom with them to the movies when my dad was on duty.

My dad befriended the pastor of the church in Old Orchard Beach where he spent so much time patrolling and being on watch.

From Gerry, August 19, 1943

This morning Father Pelletier called on me. He had great asking for you. Wanted to know if you were still working and if you'd soon stop. To top it all off, he insisted that I take five dollars to be given to you to buy a little blanket for our little "bundle of joy".

There is another great wave of transfers from our company. Here's hoping that we stay here for the duration. Most fellows are fed up with this routine, but not this uncle's nephew! [Uncle Sam]

From Gerry, September 1, 1943

Will this war ever end? I'm sure glad that we married when we did and are not still waiting for the end of the war.

From Gerry, September 22, 1943, Breakwater Farm

Here I am again. This place has been fixed up considerably since I was here before. We now have six big lamps and only six rooms to light. There's also a table to eat off and running hot water.

Today I fired on the range. Scored 189 of a possible 220 score, second highest for the day. However, this was just a practice trial. Tomorrow we shoot for record. If I can score 195 or better, I'll be an expert. I'll be trying awfully hard just for you.

Last night and tonight we played volleyball. What fun! We really have a whale of a good time.

Maybe that extra rating that they say I'm getting will come in handy. Could you use another twelve dollars per month?

My Uncle Joe and my Aunt Theresa both told me that the great radio news broadcaster Walter Winchell blew the whistle on my dad's group stationed in Maine by reporting that they were on the beaches of Maine while other units were fighting overseas! Suddenly my dad's next letter came from East Douglas, Massachusetts.

From Gerry, September 30, 1943, East Douglas, Massachusetts

It's been a hectic day. Down here they live like so many cattle in a barn.

Gee, last night I washed four pair of woolen socks and a towel hung up behind my bunk. Will you be sure to ask Bill to take care of them for me. [Socks left behind in Maine.] *It was bad enough leaving without them let alone exposing them to the danger of theft. It's hard to get good socks now.*

From Gerry, October 1, 1943,
East Douglas, Massachusetts

After evening mess, a bundle came for me. It was my socks and are they a life saver. Bill was on the job again. Nice work! Please thank him for me.

My dad was promoted to sergeant.

From Gerry, October 2, 1943,
East Douglas, Massachusetts

My mother was glad to hear of my promotion. she says that every time she had a child, my father got a raise in pay.

From Gerry, October 4, 1943,
East Douglas, Massachusetts

That dream you had was from apples. I always have a nightmare if I have an apple before bed. [My mother must have had a premonition.]

From Gerry, October 7, 1943,
East Douglas, Massachusetts

Yesterday I didn't get a chance to write. At four in the afternoon, we went into the woods and stayed all night and morning. Our meals consisted of three concentrated chocolate bars. One for each meal. Not so hot, but supposed to contain what it takes.

We were also greatly harassed by an extra overdose of tear gas. Our throats are still sore and the aches still in our eyes. However, we did a good job and are glad it's over.

Tomorrow it is to be jungle warfare. Another muddy, scratchy session of it.

My Aunt Mary's husband Bill Pease was about nine years older than my dad. He had some issues with his back and was not sent overseas.

From Gerry, October 9, 1943,
East Douglas, Massachusetts

Bill's exceptionally fortunate in remaining in camp and getting to see Mary. What'll she do when he goes to outpost or comes here to Douglas?

Today, while wearing gas masks, we marched about six miles. Down here they think of everything to make one miserable.

On October 12, Columbus Day, the soldiers rode army trucks into Boston for a Columbus Day parade. It really boosted their morale to see familiar faces and crowds to cheer them. My dad's parents and sisters as well as neighbors and friends were there.

My dad wrote, *"Our route to Boston was over many of my bicycle racing and touring courses. It brought back many fond memories."*

In November 1943, my dad wrote only two letters to my mom. He had returned to Maine after the Columbus Day parade and must have been able to see her quite often.

From Gerry, November 12, 1943, Old Orchard Beach, Maine

Gee but it's great to know that you've been feeling fine lately. I'm going to try my best to get to see you either this afternoon or tomorrow afternoon. Somehow or other, a day just isn't a day unless I've seen you. Just think, every day is another day nearer to the time when we will be together every day.

We are to have new quarters here at Old Orchard. There is everything in the one building: sleeping facilities for twenty-four men; a kitchen with range, sink, and refrigerator; showers, washroom, and continuous hot water. Some place! I'm afraid we won't be going into Saco for showers. However, you can figure that every chance I get to see you, I'll be sure to do so.

Gosh, Sweetheart, wouldn't it be swell if this all ended by the first of the year.

My sister Virginia sent me some coconut macaroon cookies that she made. If I could buy some more coconut, I'd send it to her and ask her to make some more.

Today Sheik Maffie gets presented the Soldier's Medal for pulling a girl out of the water. They'd take it away from the guy who got it last summer if they saw the way he bit a fellow out here. Not only that but he drew a knife on him and also tried to gouge out his eyes. If anyone ever tried to do that to me, I believe I wouldn't stop thrashing until he could only breathe.

From Gerry, November 30, 1943, Fort Devens, Massachusetts

We arrived in good shape and are pretty well situated. But, we won't be here very long. In fact, before the week is over, we'll be taking the train for Fort Dix.

At least it should be considerably warmer there. We should at least spend the winter there. It's only ninety miles from New York City. So I should be able to get home to you once in a while.

Tomorrow night I'm going to try to make Quincy. It would be quite a surprise to the folks and I could just about make connections if the M.P.'s leave me alone.

Well, Sweetheart, I miss you but I'll get along some how. I wanted to call you yesterday morning. However, I thought it better not to.

I did call Father Pelletier and say good-bye. He was praising you to the sky.

Lou Nota wants to skip off to Biddeford. He'll never be able to get back before six the next morning. Love's a funny thing. It makes fellows do all kinds of extraordinary things.

I was just over to the P.X. What a mad jam and rush! Pay day! Only two cigars to a customer and when I got there, all the White Owls were gone.

My grandfather Cameron smoked White Owl cigars. Undoubtedly, my dad wanted to give him some for his upcoming birthday on December fifth.

Since my arrival in this world was expected in December, my dad's letters revealed much concern for my mother, how she was feeling, and what the doctor said. His mother was preparing a bassinet for my arrival. She was an accomplished seamstress. So I'm sure it was gorgeous!

From Gerry, December 1, 1943, Fort Devens, Massachusetts

It's been easy here so far but we'll make up for it before the month is out. I'm getting prepared to go home tonight. I hope that I can make it. I should be able to if the M.P.'s and connections are good. It will be about forty miles more than I'm supposed to go, but as far as anybody knows I'll be visiting Concord. Here's hoping that I find my way back before six tomorrow morning.

I might call you if I get to Boston O.K. Your picture is right beside my bed and it sure looks good to me. I don't need it to remind me of you, but it surely does its share.

I know that your folks will take good care of you and that you'll get along, but I surely would rather be with you.

From Gerry, December 2, 1943, Fort Devens, Massachusetts

It was great getting home last night. The folks were out to a wake, but a telephone call brought them home quickly. Everything is ship shape. Wait 'til you see the bassinet. You'll really go big for it!

I bought a box of cigars for my dad and he was quite well satisfied.

Well, I got back here at four o'clock this morning and up at five thirty. It is now ten thirty P.M. My head is just about ready to bump my chest every time I put the pen on the paper.

Bill is sitting opposite me writing Mary. We are told that there won't be any mail go in or out so we are asked why we are writing, but that doesn't stop us.

Well, Sweetheart, I've got to be making bed check and it isn't going to be an easy job. So it goes.

All the boys miss Maine already!

From Gerry, December 3, 1943,
Fort Devens, Massachusetts

Well tomorrow is the day. Tonight is the last one here. I'm going down town, call you, and try a little shopping.

Bill's going to town with me but he's afraid that if he calls Mary, she'll break down like she did when he went to Framingham.

From Gerry, December 6, 1943, Fort Dix, New Jersey

We finally arrived here after an out of the way fifteen hour train ride through Troy and Albany, New York. We are now living in tents. Things aren't so good, but they could be worse.

There is a big airfield right near us. All day and night we hear and see big B17 flying fortresses taking off, landing, and flying in all directions.

Right now it is drizzling and raining. Last night was rather chilly for one used to sleeping indoors. My feet were freezing all night. You wouldn't let that happen, would you, Sweetheart?

We have a little wood stove, the simplest one I've ever seen—no grates, bottom, drafts, or anything. It's just like a tent in itself.

Tonight Bill, Brownie, and I went to the show. The picture was "North Star"—not so bad, but still war stuff, and of course a certain amount of propaganda.

While in Devens, I bought a new frame for your picture. It gives it additional class.

Well, Sweetheart, I'm waiting to be at your side. It'll be swell to be with you again. Down here it seems as though half my life has been taken away. I really need you. This penance will make our reunion all the happier.

The B17 Flying Fortress, a four-engine strategic bomber, flown by the United States Army Air Force in World War II.

From Gerry, December 7, 1943, Fort Dix, New Jersey

Today Tom McHugh and I started schooling on physical training. We are to go for two hours a morning for two weeks. The course is the latest thing from Washington. It is designed to really put the boys in shape. Wow! Are my leg muscles in knots tonight. It'll take the rest of the week just to loosen them up.

We've been very busy cleaning up and fixing up. It seems that every time we move, we get all the dirty work. Bill hates it here. He's really disgusted.

Oh well! Anything is better than being across. At least it only takes a couple of days for a letter to be delivered. No mail for me today. That'll never do. It seems I'll have to write a lot myself to make sure that I get answers every day.

They said that Regimental Headquarters is working on passes for us and they will have good news. Here's hoping. Gosh! It would seem like heaven to be with you again. If we did get forty-eight hour passes, I'd only be able to spend twenty-four with you. But every minute would be enjoyed to the utmost.

Two years today. [He is referring to Pearl Harbor.] *Gee! Wouldn't it be swell if it were all over by next summer and we could really enjoy married life?*

From Gerry, December 8, 1943, Fort Dix, New Jersey

Well it's another day and another dollar, but the only satisfaction is that it's another day nearer to the end of all this, and just that much sooner to being with you. Someday, Sweetheart, we'll be able to laugh at all of this. However, it certainly will help us to be even closer to one another.

There is a chance that they won't allow me to leave here after the baby is born. So when it does happen, please follow these procedures. Ask someone to send a telegram to me, and also to notify the Red Cross which is located directly in front of the shoe shop, and they in turn can notify the Red Cross here. By following those procedures, the cause could be better put over. Gee, Heaven knows I've been looking forward to it long enough.

Maybe you think that the Doc is right when he says the fifteenth, but I'll still bet that it'll be closer to the twenty-fourth.

Don't let me down now. It'll have to be a boy or else I'll have to shell out a dollar and be faced with the charge that I'm not man enough to be the father of a boy. However, come what may, I'll be tickled and proud, and I know you will too.

Gee, Sweetheart, I can hardly wait to see you again. Right now and from now on you are all that matters. If I didn't have you, I wouldn't give a darn.

Gee my legs are sore and stiff. Those two hours of physical exercises every day are kind of hard to break into.

Well, Sweetheart, write soon and as often as you can, because I'm pining away.

My father and Uncle Bill somehow made it to Maine to celebrate my mother's twenty-third birthday on December 10th.

From Gerry, December 13, 1943, Fort Dix, New Jersey

We arrived here O.K. this morning. Was in bed at four only to get up again at five. It took longer to get from New York to Trenton than it did to go from Biddeford to Boston.

Mary's condition [She was pregnant with my cousin Francis] *showed up in her eyes. I'm glad for her. You two sure are a great comfort to one another. That's one arrangement that's nice about our set up.*

That was a tasty cake Mary made for you. Two different times on the way back we enjoyed eating it with ice cream. It's a good thing we had it because we didn't get a chance to eat anything else.

We can't always control our circumstances in life, but we can control our attitude in the midst of whatever circumstances come our way. I believe my father maintained a positive attitude.

From Gerry, December 17, 1943, Fort Dix, New Jersey

Gee, but the fellows are complaining about things in general. I get a big kick out of it. Even before I came down here, I'd made up my mind that I was going to see the funny side of things. I really bellow at the fellows when I hear them squawking.

From Gerry, December 20, 1943, Fort Dix, New Jersey

I've got to get rid of my personal equipment, handy knick-knacks, etc. They're really cutting us down on everything. What a job! I'm so Scotch I hate to part with anything.

Bill and I get together every so often. We're afraid we might be separated.

On December 21, 1943 I made my entrance into this world. My dad was given four days leave. He arrived in Biddeford on Christmas Eve. He borrowed my Grandfather Colpitts' car to transport my mom and me home from the hospital.

He later wrote, "It was swell driving home from the hospital—just the three of us starting out on our family threshold."

He went out Christmas Eve and bought a baby carriage and filled it with presents for everyone. I was told that one store in Biddeford remained open just for him to do all his shopping.

Because my mom and dad were strong Catholics from very devoted Catholic families, my dad had me baptized with my Aunt Mary and Uncle Bill as godparents. They were very devoted to me for the remainder of their long lives. I grew up enjoying close relationships with their three children Francis, Peggy, and Terry.

After emotional good-byes in Maine, my dad made a stop in Quincy, Massachusetts to say good-by to his family, and he was on his way back to the Army.

CHAPTER FOUR

1944–The Front Lines

As 1944 DAWNED, my dad left Fort Dix and was on his way to Fort Meade, Maryland.

From Gerry, January 3, 1944, Fort Meade, Maryland

Gee, that was a swell note you wrote to me. I was really glad to read it. You knew all the time that my recent visit was probably all that you'd see of me for some time. But you never can tell, so never get discouraged and give up hope.

Gee, they are surely shaking us down now. I'm sending home my little handbag.

Bill is in another outfit now. He has to have a little fixing up. He has some health issues. I don't know whether he's said anything to Mary yet, but if he does catch up with us it'll be some time from now.

Well, Sweetheart, things are moving exceptionally fast here. All indications are that we will be well on our way to our overseas destination before this month is out. Please don't be worried, Fran, I'm not.

My dad went on to explain the finances including insurance, war bonds, etc., so that my mom and I would be well provided for within his means.

You and the baby are so sweet that I'm still reeling from the thrill of it. Gee, but I feel proud and happy. What a reunion it'll be when we are all together again.

From Gerry, January 5, 1944, Fort Meade, Maryland

Well, I haven't the slightest idea where I'll be a month from now, but it'll be many miles further than I've ever been from you before. But my heart will be closer than ever.

From Gerry, January 7, 1944, Fort Meade, Maryland

Before me I have four of your letters. If I can receive that many every week that I'm away, things will be swell. With you and the baby living for me, it'll be easier to live for you.

Thank God that I'm able to leave feeling that everything is right and that He is with me.

From what you write of our Mary, I gather that she is sharpening up fast. I hope that she'll keep you busy and consoled while I'm away.

There sure has been a lot happen in forty-three, and from the looks of things, we'll see plenty in forty-four. We surely are living in a history making era.

I'll bet the baby is getting better meals than I'm getting. I'm telling you, Sweetheart, the next time you see me, I'll be lucky if I weigh as much as I did when you fell in love with me.

Have you gained all your strength back yet? Guess you must have because that last time you hugged me was the tightest yet, and that was just after you came from the hospital.

Don't be surprised or uneasy if you don't receive another letter from me for as long as a month. We don't know what the orders will be or where we'll be. So look for the bright side of possibilities. However, don't let up on your writing. If you don't hear from me, it'll only be because we won't be able to write or we won't be in a place to mail letters. So don't think that I'm forgetting you or neglecting to write.

Gee, I hope that your folks won't tire of having you and the baby around. Don't let your mother do too much.

Even without you working, we should have quite a sum to start our own home and business if things so shape up. Well, anyhow, I probably will have plenty of time to think, and in so doing, be able to provide you with more than the necessities.

So, Sweetheart, keep your spirits up. Things won't be too tough. We've got what it takes. Father Mac says we shouldn't take our hats off to anybody.

From Gerry, January 9, 1944, Fort Meade, Maryland

Gosh but I'm glad that you are enjoying the baby so much. It was very thoughtful of you to have invited my folks to meet their granddaughter. I'll bet they will really get a thrill out of it.

Tell Mary not to worry about Bill. If he does have an operation, it'll only be a minor one and at that the best cure. He'll probably even get a furlough afterwards. If so, send him that railroad ticket which I sent to you. I'm not able to see Bill, so say, "so long" for me.

My dad always inquired about me in these letters. He wrote:

I don't suppose that you know how much the baby weighs now. But I'll bet that you can practically see her grow. You've probably taught her to recognize you already. What color are her eyes going to be?

Sweetheart, you are a brick. I have never known you to complain or ask for anything ever since I've known you.

Don't forget to kiss the baby for me. I'm hoping to be home for her birthday celebration. [I wasn't even a month old.]

On January 15, my dad informed my mom that from that point on his letters would be 100% censored. About two or three sentences were cut out of that letter. However, he assured my mom that her letters would not be censored and that she could feel free to say anything to him. He wrote:

The tone of your letters tells me how thrilled you are with our precious daughter. It makes me feel so good to know that you can be happy even with things the way they are.

When I think back on our married life, it has been short and only a scanty part time existence. But, Sweet, every moment has been golden. It is wonderful to be able to look forward to the blossoming in full of such a beautiful bud. Wouldn't it be something to fulfill the Golden Anniversary that our friend Father Clancy bid we enjoy. Being away from you is hard; but by looking back and then on a future based on such a past, I believe that I could endure anything.

From Gerry, January 18, 1944, Fort Meade, Maryland
[Concerning the food]

The boys are complaining about hot dogs. We had them for breakfast, dinner, and supper. Of course, they had to be of an unknown quality. If they show up again for breakfast, I don't think anyone will eat. Otherwise, the food has been fairly good. No one could complain that he didn't get enough to eat.

The Catholic chaplain wrote to my mom that her soldier "looked well and in good spirits."

He has proven himself a true soldier of Christ by going to confession and receiving Holy Communion during the time he spent here.

Suddenly the letters from my dad stopped and a "V-Mail" (short for Victory Mail) arrived.

V-Mail was an ingenious mail process that allowed World War II military personnel stationed abroad, and their families and friends stateside, to securely correspond with each other. Letters were written on special paper, then after censoring of any possible sensitive information, it was copied to microfilm. When the film arrived at its destination, the negative would be enlarged, printed, and finally delivered to its recipient. V-Mail reduced thousands of tons of shipping space that would have been taken up by regular mail thereby freeing it for needed war materials.

From Gerry, February 8, 1944, Italy

This is my first letter to you in three weeks. So don't be looking for any letters previous to this. This is my first chance to write. So, Sweetheart, don't be too disappointed if you don't hear from me regularly. It'll mean that I'm on the move, or in a place where a letter can't be censored and mailed or for lack of time or light. As it is now, I'm in a tent sharing one candle with seven other fellows.

Well, Fran, I'm safe and sound in Italy. I've already visited Africa and [censored] and got a good glimpse of the [censored]. The country here is beautiful. It's just like April back home. The people are nice but they've suffered much because of the war.

In a book about my father's regiment, my mom had inserted a note to me:

Your father was shipped overseas about January 20, 1944 headed for north Africa, but due to heavy casualties in Italy at the Rapido River Disaster some of the ships in the convoy were ordered to Italy, and it was at that point that your dad became part of the 141st Infantry.

From Gerry, February 13, 1944, Italy

How's my Sweetheart? My Valentine? And our little Mary? My thoughts are continuously of you. I'm always looking forward to being back with you.

Things aren't so easygoing over here. The land is almost entirely mountainous and so we really get a workout.

Don't think that I'm forgetting or neglecting to write. This is only my second opportunity. Possibly, I'll get more chances soon.

Well, I'm now in the so called famous "Thirty-Sixth" Division. It's part of General Clark's Fifth Army. So you can follow our progress in the news.

Gee, Fran, I miss you terribly. I didn't get to Mass today. There wasn't any. I hope that you did and prayed for me because I'm going to need your prayers. I surely hope that this is all over this summer and that we'll be together next fall.

The Allies sure are on the move. I've seen almost every nation represented.

141st Infantry Regiment Unit Insignia

The soldiers of the 141st Infantry in World War II:

- were among the first American troops to land in Europe, to enter Rome, and to land on the coast of Southern France
- the first of the 36th Division troops to enter Germany
- experienced 361 days of combat 137 days in Italy, 204 days in France, 17 days in Germany and 4 days in Austria.
- sustained more than 6,000 casualties in World War II, including 1,126 killed, approximately 5,000 wounded, and over 500 missing in action.
- received 2,614 awards and decorations

On February 17 my dad wrote that he hadn't received any mail in over a month.

From Gerry, February 23, 1944, Italy

Never before have I longed to be with you so much. We've never been apart so long. It seems as though every breath I take is another one towards seeing you and the baby. It's a real tough job I've got over here. So, Sweetheart, pray extra hard and we'll be together again. I'm hoping that it'll be this year.

Have my folks been up to see little Mary yet? I'll bet they'll fall in love with her right away.

Gee, Fran, we sure were fortunate in meeting when we did, marrying and becoming parents etc. Everything worked out perfectly. To have you and the baby to come to is a real incentive. It means so much to us.

My mother and me on a cold winter's day in Maine

At Last I Know My Father

From Gerry, March 2, 1944, Italy

Just a year ago we were anxiously awaiting that great day. Then everything worked out perfectly. Now we are waiting to be together again. It's always something. However, my hopes and faith are high and I'm thinking that this time next year is going to find "we three" in our happy little home.

I see where the government is going to loan money to veterans who were forced to liquidate their businesses because of going into the service. Perhaps I'll take advantage of that.

Anyhow, Sweetheart, you had better enjoy Maine now because I'm thinking that your little corner with the white house trimmed in green won't be there.

When my mom finally got her own house in 1970, it was a corner house which she had painted white with green trim!

It's getting dark. I'll have to make up my straw sack and blankets.

That "Sunny Italy" expression is the bunk! It's been raining practically every day since we arrived here. We even weathered a heavy snowstorm.

My parents first wedding anniversary was March 6, 1944. My dad wrote my mother the day before.

From Gerry, March 5, 1944, Italy

Here it is the first Saturday in March, only it isn't the sixth yet. I've had all kinds of pleasant memories running through my head. When I get back to you , we'll have to go on another honeymoon. So, be thinking of some place that you'd like to go.

Today I bought four bottles of coco-cola. That is the first I've had and they'll have to do me for the week. Twice a month we can buy two bars of candy. The other day I went to town. If it wasn't for nuts, apples, and oranges, I'd have starved. There just wasn't anything to eat.

While I was at the front lines, I didn't eat hardly enough to keep me going. With that ordeal and the trip over, I managed to lose about fifteen pounds. However, I'm gaining it back now.

Today I went to two Masses—one for Italians and one for soldiers. I hadn't been for three Sundays. The Italian women sing the Rosary. It is quite an impressive chant. I'm ashamed of myself. I didn't even know it was Lent.

Well, tomorrow is the day. I'm looking for something special to happen. When the church bells in the local village ring, I'll interpret them in celebration of our Wonderful Wedding. Gee, Sweetheart, it doesn't seem possible that the picture I carry of my bride is already a year old. Now I'm waiting for one of you and our little Mary.

Gosh it is raining again. What a miserable stretch of it we've had. My shoes haven't been dry for three weeks.

On March 6, the actual date of my parents' first wedding anniversary, my dad wrote again.

From Gerry, March 6, 1944, Italy

This morning I had a pleasant surprise. Out of a clear sky, the first sergeant told me that I was going to the rest camp. So here I am for five days of relaxing, recreation, and entertainment. At least my mind will occupied until I get a letter from you. And surely after another five days, my mail should be catching up with me.

Today you should have received a box of roses. I'll be interested to know if it arrived in good shape and on time. I ordered them back in the States. Next year I hope that we'll be celebrating together. We surely will have a lot to celebrate. [Unfortunately, my dad was scammed on the roses. My mom received carnations instead!]

It sure is a relief to have my feet on a floor, not ankle deep in mud and water; and to be writing at a desk with electric lights.

There is a free tour to Pompeii. I might take it in.

Every time that I think of a year ago, I get lost and it's hard to get back to the reality of this existence. Ho! Hum! It's always darkest before the dawn. The dawn can't be too far off.

Another ten days and it'll be three years of service for me. But I've nothing to regret because I'd not have met you and my life would have still been empty.

In a conversation I had with my dad's brother Bill about two years ago, he told me that my dad had been wounded in Italy and that he didn't want my mother to know. I don't know if that is the reason that my dad was at the rest camp at this time.

From Gerry, March 6, 1944, Italy [the rest camp]

I've been having quite a time of it. There's a beautiful church here in town. There are shows and movies every afternoon and evening. We have improvised beds on which to sleep, good meals, no work, and easy chairs to relax as much as we please. This rest camp is a great place for the fellows who have been on edge at the front to get back to normal.

I went on that trip to Pompeii that I previously mentioned. It was a city of vice. There is no doubt in my mind that it was the wrath of God that caused its destruction.

I'm more than anxious to get back to my outfit because I believe that there'll be letters from you.

There is a very large portion of children to the total population. Most of them are happy and fairly neat. However, there are others who are barefoot, undernourished, and dirty. One pities them and wonders what kind of parents theirs must be.

The Germans have done as much as they could to make the utilities, etc. useless to us. They even went to the extent of blowing the ends off every piece of rail. All the electric power lines are devastated.

The man who predicted the end of the last war says Easter Sunday for this one. Hope he's right. What a glorious occasion that would be.

My dad didn't receive any mail until March 13. After that he encouraged my mom to try airmail and to send him some six cent stamps so he could do likewise.

From Gerry, March 17, 1944, Italy

As to what I'm doing, I can't very well say much. Besides, it wouldn't be interesting. Then again, I'll have to have something to tell you when I get back to living with you. Lately, I've been eating well and outside of little colds bound to occur from so much excessive wet weather, I've been feeling good. There are only two things that bother me. One is lonesomeness and the other is when am I going to be with you.

My dad inquired of me frequently and commented on what others wrote of me.

The reports on little Mary have been more than satisfying. I surely feel proud of her and you and my little family. What a head start we've got on most other young couples. When I return I'll be all reared up to go places. Wonder how little Mary will react when she first gazes on her "Old Gent."

From Gerry, March 19, 1944, Italy

Spring will be here this week and then watch the boys over here get at those Nazis! At least the end of the war is closer than ever.

With spring will come the anniversary of our meeting. What a happy day that was for me. I knew then that we'd pair up. All this time apart should make our coming life together all the more pleasant.

From Gerry, March 21, 1944, Italy

So your father gets a thrill out of holding his most recent kin. So would I. It wouldn't be right if she didn't receive some masculine attention.

You mentioned hoping that it'd be possible for me to be home for little Mary's birthday celebration. To tell the truth, I still believe that I will be. Most of us feel that everything will be over, over here before Fall.

So our "prize package" is over twelve pounds and cutting teeth. Gee, that's swell. Good news to receive on the day she's three months old.

From Gerry, March 23, 1944, Italy

It makes me happy every time I think of you and the baby. I'm so glad that I have you both to come home to.

Well, Sweetheart, everything is OK with me. So don't be worrying. Everything will come out OK and for the best. Remember that you're the greatest incentive I could possibly have.

From Gerry, March 26, 1944, Italy

I'm enjoying some American recordings, a nice hall, and a table and chair—even though it took an hour and a half's waiting for the seat.

We are all waiting to hear that the Russians have reached Berlin. Seems as if this drastic affair has lasted long enough.

Well, Fran, I'm fine and all I can think of is getting home to you. Keep your hopes high. I still think that it'll be this year.

From Gerry, March 29, 1944, Italy

This should reach you Easter Saturday. Wouldn't it be wonderful if this war could be all over by then. Anyhow, Sweetheart, rejoice just the same because Easter is the greatest day that we have. It even surmounts Christmas.

Well, Fran, I'm in the best of health and I'm contented. Things are running smoothly and the time is going by fast.

The invasion should take place any day and then things should end quickly. Never despair, our life together has strong roots and will survive through whatever might be thrown against it.

From Gerry, March 31, 1944, Italy

The next time you have a hot fudge sundae don't forget to eat a little extra for me. Remember how I used to consume a second for my brother Bill.

Poor Bill Pease is having his hard times. Just think, there are all kinds of fellows over here who wish that they could have something like that to keep them from the front. That's how things are!

Gee, I sure am missing something in not being able to watch our little Mary. I'll have a real surprise awaiting me when next I see her.

Today I was notified that I'm now a Staff Sergeant.

I'm glad to learn that the baby isn't tongue tied. That wouldn't be so nice. That's something that most people never think of.

All my love to you and our little Mary.

In a letter dated April 1, 1944, my father mentioned that he had five ambitions. One day, on one of my mother's last visits to my home, she told me that my dad had five items on his personal prayer list. He prayed for good health, work, a wife and family, a home, and eternal salvation for all.

From Gerry, April 4, 1944, Italy

Does the little tot still pull her dress up? [Dad, I was only three months old!]

The more she grows, the busier she'll keep you.

Tough on Bill Pease having to undergo the same operation again. But, it'll be worth it if he can get to be with Mary when their baby is born like I was able to be with you. Gee, that was a real break. Everything went off perfectly.

Tell your mom that I appreciate what she is doing for me. Tell her that I'm studying Italian so that I can interpret when Mrs. Alasantro, [my mom's next door neighbor], *comes around.*

Tasker Street, the road in Saco, Maine where my mom lived, was not paved. When the snow melted in the spring, the road was muddy and full of potholes. My dad inquired how she ever managed with the baby carriage on such a road.

From Gerry, April 9, 1944, Italy

Easter Sunday, the greatest day of the year! Next Easter I expect to be with you and Mary. This morning I went to Mass at a beautiful Italian church. It is a real peaceful church. It is a real peaceful day. I hope that you find it the same way. Everything is getting ready to bloom. Some of the blossoms and flowers already have. There are many flowers resembling our violets, daisies, buttercups, etc.

It tickled me to receive word from my mother that my folks had been up to see you. She says that the baby is a sweetheart, just like a real nice doll. The weather was fine and they enjoyed every bit of the trip.

Gee, they'd better hurry and get this over with. I want to be on my way back in September. If I have to spend a fourth year in this army, I feel I'll never be good for any life—even this. I'm all fed up with not having my freedom. It's really worth fighting for.

I could have gone to town this afternoon, but I didn't care to. I only want to go back and be with you, Sweetheart.

At Last I Know My Father

From Gerry, April 10, 1944, Italy

Lately I've seen some swell little kids. I can hardly wait to see little Mary. You'll have to get "on the ball" with some snapshots. Well, Sweetheart, everything is going OK and each day a day sooner to our glorious reunion. So I guess we can't complain.

From Gerry, April 13 and 14, 1944, Italy

If the baby keeps getting out, she'll be tanned like her father already is.

If little Mary is imitating coughs and laughs already, she'll soon be hooting at trains.

I've been fortunate in being able to attend Mass frequently.

So Henry Ford said that it'd be over in two months. Sounds good to me.

Well, Sweetheart, I'm gradually reducing. Do you think that you'll be able to recognize me coming down Tasker Street?

Virginia, [my dad's sister], *tells me that I should be with little Mary now because she maybe needs a father's stern hand.*

Every day is another one nearer our reunion. So it won't be too bad waiting.

From Gerry, April 17, 1944, Italy

Everything has been going fine. I hope that you haven't been worrying about me. They sure keep us busy. *I don't think I'll ever catch up with the letters I now owe. Gee, you've been doing a great job this month.*

If I were there I'd show little Mary how to really smash up rattles.

This morning I heard "A Sleepy Lagoon". That's what was playing the night I met you. What pleasant memories! I wonder if I'll still be able to dance. It's been so long I'm rusty at everything. But, my love for you is very keen.

From Gerry, April 21, 1944, Italy

I've been making up for your not being able to get to church so often, even to the extent of missions. I've been especially fortunate in that respect.

Well, if Henry Ford is right, this will all be over in one more month. But if that invasion doesn't take place real soon, I wouldn't even want to guess.

I'm so tired I can't think. Well, Fran, maybe it won't be long before we'll be together and not need to write letters. It seems near, but still far away.

I had ice cream on top of cherry pie today! It was swell.

From Gerry, April 23, 1944, Italy

Gee, we've had more than a month of spring and nothing has happened in the way of an invasion. Something had better pop real soon.

Well, Sweetheart, here's hoping that I get a letter from you tomorrow. One from you makes a day complete.

I've seen a little more of Italy. The churches sure are beautiful and have grand old histories. I saw an all gold chalice made from a thousand dollars worth of gold. It's over five hundred years old and beautifully carved. The old pastor just recently dug it up together with gold vestments which were buried to keep the Germans from getting them.

I'm able to go to Mass about every day.

Don't worry about me. I'll get along OK. Just take good care of yourself and the baby and it'll not be long before we'll be together.

From Gerry, April 25, 1944, Italy

Tonight I hit the jackpot for nine letters dating from yours of January 13th to yours of April 11th and my brother Bill's of the 12th. [Bill was in the U.S. Army stationed in India at that time.]

He's having some time of it eating shark, goat, and camel meat with the British.

So you have enough clothes for three babies. We'll have to do something about that.

My love for you mounts greater with every passing day.

From Gerry, April 27, 1944, Italy

Gee, I hate this army life just as much as ever; but, there doesn't seem to be much that I can do about it. Guess it's always darkest before the dawn.

From Gerry, April 30, 1944, Italy

Gosh I don't know what I'll do if this thing doesn't hurry up and get over with. I sure miss you now. You're on my mind more constantly than ever. At every meal I eat, there is a little girl who looks enough like you to be your daughter. She waits for the leftovers. I sure enjoy looking at her. I can see you in every look.

I hope you'll be proud on Mother's Day. You've just as much right to as anybody. And what better name could you have given the baby!

From Gerry, May 4, 1944, Italy

Those snapshots certainly were a sight for sore eyes. Gee, Sweetheart, you look swell and so happy with the baby who has grown so much.

I'm sorry that I'm not always able to write to you every day, but sometimes I'm not where that can be done. Like the last three days, for example.

I've been having a whale of a time playing volley ball and softball. That along with all the mountain climbing around here has been streamlining yours truly.

Gosh the baby will be five and six months old before we realize it. She ought to be showing a tooth any day now.

Remember this is the month that we met. What a glorious occasion that was. Wait'll the next time, you should wear a steel vest so that I don't crush you.

Well, the invasion had better come this month, or I won't be home in September.

At Last I Know My Father

From Gerry, May 8, 1944, Italy

My dad writes me that you are a very indulgent mother. I know that you are and I hope that it won't be too long before more children will know you as such. He also says that both you and your sister Mary have a swell set up and that you are as happy as can be expected without your mates.

Gee, the mosquitoes are biting and this is where they spread malaria. The grease on the paper is repellant.

Now I'm anxious for some more snapshots. Only the next batch, make sure that there's a couple of you. Don't let the baby hog it all!

How about sending me a package of something good to eat? All the other fellows in the tent have been getting them and I feel like a sponge having nothing to offer them. I understand that you must show the postal clerk the request. So show them this paragraph.

Things had better start happening in a hurry if I'm going to fulfill my date with you this fall. After all, I'll have to be at the baby's birthday celebration.

There's been a decided change in the weather. So much so, that I've removed the long drawers and have already been in swimming.

This country is about thirty years behind ours.

I hope that I'll see you before that new outfit of yours gets worn out. I'll bet that you're a knockout in it.

From Gerry, May 11, 1944, Italy

Everything has been going swell lately; however, it probably won't be long before I'll be needing your prayers.

Gee, the water was great. Reminded me of the beach the last two years. I'm hoping to get in some more swimming.

This country is nothing but gardens and mountains. The gardens are now in full bloom and really something to see. The people work very hard at farming. It is quite a sight to see them all setting out in the wagons early in the morning and the constant parade of horses, mules, donkeys, wagons, and "Dagos" returning from the fields at sundown.

I've got that European tan that they sing about.

From Gerry, May 14, 1944, Italy

Here it is Mother's Day, and for you the first one in which you are to be included among the honored souls and beings. Dearest one, I wish that I could be there to pay tribute and show my appreciation to you not only today, but always.

The attacks have started here again and it probably won't be too long before we are participating in a great decisive victory. So, Fran, keep praying. We really have reason to.

It did things to me when I learned that your eyes filled up every time my name was mentioned. I hope that I'll see them do the same as many times because of joyous incidents.

Gee. Fran, it doesn't seem as though this war can last much longer. I've just got to see you in 1944. We can't have a vacant year in our life together.

I'm signing off wishing that I could express some of the vast amount of love that I've been storing for you.

From Gerry, May 18, 1944, Italy

Today is Ascension Thursday. I'm in hopes of getting to Mass. However, some of these higher-ups don't seem to care one way or another.

I'll be waiting to see you in your new blue outfit. How much do you weigh?

Do you think that the baby will be afraid of me?

From Gerry, May 23, 1944, Italy

Please don't think that anything has happened or that I'm forgetting you because I haven't written so much of late. As I told you before, there will be times when I can't write regularly.

So the little tot has shown her temper. You'll have to sit on her. Just ignore her when she tries that.

Funny thing about mosquito netting, her daddy has to sleep under it too. We take all the precautions against malaria.

Well, Sweetheart, I'm as well as ever and in good spirits. Victory in Italy is taking place. There's still a good chance of my seeing you this fall. Remember me to all.

From Gerry, May 24, 1944, Italy

I'm feeling as good as ever and am ready for any eventuality. I'm constantly thinking of you and our little Mary and am so glad that you have her. It doesn't seem as though the Germans can hold out on this front much longer. So don't forget to save me a couple of ears of corn.

From Gerry, May 25, 1944, Italy

Frances, Sweetheart, just think next week will be two years that we've enjoyed living for one another. Gee, I wish that there were some way to celebrate. Possibly there will be, who knows? Even though I'm at war, they have been the two happiest years of my life.

I'll be waiting to hear how much the baby weighs. She must be a bouncing bambino. Can she sit up or crawl yet?

So they sliced up one of my letters. Oh well, there is so much that we can't say that we're all stuck for something to write about. But I'd have not written it if I'd thought that it would be of any value to the enemy or have given the censor any trouble.

Well, Fran, here's another month almost gone by. The next month will tell whether or not I'll be home in the fall. With every passing day there is a certain satisfaction. So just keep on patiently waiting and it'll not be in vain. My dad says that your faith and courage are admirable.

According to what I have learned about the history of World War II, the American soldiers entered Rome on June 4, 1944. By the summer, Rome was free. It was spared bombing. The American soldiers got their combat experience in Italy in 1944. The Italian campaign was successful and the German army had been pushed back.

From Gerry, June 7, 1944, Italy

I don't know how long it has been since I last wrote. This has been my first chance. So don't be worried if it's a long time before the next one. I've put in much temporal suffering and God is with us. I'm in good shape and about thirty pounds lighter. You'd better get in a lot of cooking because I'm going to need it. I still intend to be home for a feed of corn. Right now I can't think of anything in particular that I need. But any packages with something good to eat in them will surely come in handy.

The more I travel in Italy, the more beautiful are the sights and country and the people seem nicer.

I am writing with a German fountain pen. Ha! Ha! It can't last much longer. Just occupy your attention with the baby and I'll be home before you know it. Then won't we have a lot to talk about and do.

From Gerry, June 13, 1944, Italy

There hasn't been much mail reach me lately so please excuse any appearances of ignorance as to what may have taken place with you lately.

1944–The Front Lines

If I remember correctly, this is only the second or third letter I've written this month. I'm not letting you down, Sweetheart. There are ample reasons.

What do you think of our successes here? Most of the prisoners say that the war is over as far as their outfits are concerned. Most of them are forced to fight by German officers. Our enemy consists of Poles, Serbs, Austrians, Russians, Siberians, etc. Those Nazi Germans sure are mean anti-Christ illegitimate militarists.

This is definitely a just war and Christianity's final struggle. The boys who have been spared from casualty so far are, by far, the most righteous.

My hunch is that the next month will have seen an armistice before it is time for another two new moons. So I'll stick to my idea, (with the help of God), that I'll be heading for you in September.

So, Fran, pray fervently for that and also in thanksgiving for what has already taken place.

Of about two thousand men who crossed a river, I was the only one who fell in. Got soaked and also a laugh out of all who saw me.

Well, I'm still in good shape and very much determined to stay that way.

The more we travel, the better the natives are, and the more we like this country. I'll be able to talk you deaf, dumb, and blind.

At Last I Know My Father

HEADQUARTERS 36TH INFANTRY DIVISION
APO #36, U. S. Army

16 June 1944

MEN OF THE 36TH INFANTRY (TEXAS) DIVISION

It is with great pride that I contratulate you on your magnificent achievements in battle to date.

Nine months ago you landed on the hostile beaches of PAESTUM, the vanguard of your country's Army, to crash the gates of Hitler's European Fortress. In that, your first action of the war, fighting courageously against well-trained enemy forces of long combat experience, you established the first American beachhead on the European Continent, the first to be established anywhere by Americans against German opposition.

For this achievement alone, you have a right to feel justly proud.

Later on, while subject to hardships that have never been exceeded by any troops anywhere, you drove the enemy from his well-organized, stoutly defended positions in the hill masses of CAMINO and SUMMUCRO; from MT. MAGGIORE, MT. LUNGO, MT. ROTUNDO and SAN PIETRO. You punished him severely. His losses in men and materiel were great. Throughout this period of bitter winter weather, under the most adverse conditions of climate and terrain, you maintained a cheerfulness and enthusiasm far superior to that of your enemy.

Then came your gallant effort on the RAPIDO. Let us bow our heads in reverence to the fallen comrades who crossed that bitterly contested stream and put up a great, if losing, fight--as great from the standpoint of sheer gallantry and determination as any recorded in the annals of our Armed Forces.

At CASSINO and CASTELLONE RIDGE you were severely tested. You suffered losses, but you captured vital high ground from the strongly entrenched enemy, and held it throughout a month of hard fighting.

After a well-deserved rest you were ordered to attack again--at a critical time and at a critical place near VELLETRI, to break the stronghold of the enemy defenses east of ROME. History will record forever your outstanding success. In a week of brilliant maneuvers and relentless assaults on one position after another, VELLETRI, ROCCA DI PAPA, MARINO and beyond, you killed and captured well over three thousand of the enemy; routed him from his strong, well-organized positions and drove him across the TIBER in disorder.

Your brilliant performance on that famous battlefield was a major contribution in the capture of the first European capital to be recovered from Nazi occupation. For your magnificent accomplishment here, General Marshall sent a personal message of congratulation to you and to me. The German Army is still reeling from your blows. The relentless pressure of your attacks will substantially shorten the duration of the war. Your victorious march through the streets of the cities of your enemy cannot be long delayed.

FRED L. WALKER
Major General, U. S. Army
Commanding

This picture of my dad was taken in Italy in June, 1944 soon after the fall of Rome. He had lost thirty pounds. He attributed the bruise over his eye to shell concussion.

From Gerry, June 21, 1944, Italy

Haven't been able to write before this. You under-stand why. I'm in good health except that I lost thirty pounds and don't think I'll ever catch up with my rest or sleep. There were eight days before the fall of Rome that I managed a total of four hours sleep. I'd just as soon not gain back the weight. Seems that I'm just about what I should be.

So glad that you're able to go visiting with the baby and that she is so observing and makes such a hit. Hope she's good and not spoiled.

Well, Sweetheart, my guess is that the Germans will be done for before my birthday, [August 16], gets around.

Gosh, now is the time to be in Maine. Summer is here and that's the only time that place is worthwhile.

I haven't been paid for a couple of months. So there hasn't been any extra sent to you.

I hope that you are as happy as can be until I return, and then everything should be wonderful.

From Gerry, June 23, 1944, Italy

At last I've a little breathing spell and right now I hope to answer some of your letters of the past two months. It sure does me good to hear from you. I'm really in need of your letters. Keep them coming — every day, if possible.

All I desire is to be with you and our Mary. How happy we shall be if God sees us to a reunion. A happy family life is the only one.

I've seen a great deal. Many things I'll never forget. Other things I want to forget, and some that I've already forgotten. Possibly I'll have changed slightly from what I was before. I know that I've aged, been boosted in faith, and possibly grown a little more serious. Let's hope that everything will have been for the better.

As far as how things are going, the Lord has been with me all the time and I've many thanksgivings to offer. Then to all those who have been praying for me, their prayers have so far been most helpful.

Gee, Fran, you're so busy now with only one, what'll you ever do with me and a half a dozen others around? You'll have to learn a lot of short-cuts.

Well, how many teeth does our little one sport now? She ought to go for about four. Gosh, I sure am aching for a look at her. How about those six by four and one half (or there about) facial photos I asked for—one of you and one of her. You'll have to get on the ball. Every time that some other chap gets a picture of his wife or child, it makes me green with envy.

It looks as though you'll have to wait until next year for your swimming lessons. You surely are missing something. [My mother never did learn to swim.]

Thanks for sending the sugar, etc. I haven't received it yet, but I'm living in expectation. You would be doing another good deed if you sent another soon. Keep 'em coming, Sweetheart. I'll put a request in every letter if they want that much red tape.

There was a while when the going was so tough that if it wasn't for wine, there'd have been five days that I think I'd have dropped from exhaustion. But I haven't tasted any since that was worthwhile drinking.

Did you ever give the baby a good spanking and ignore her for a while? Seems as if she makes a nuisance of herself quite often. Can't have her turning out like others we've seen.

Yesterday, a fellow gave me a swell set of Rosary beads. The beads are flat brown and the Crucifix opens up and contains a piece of earth from the cata-combs. One day I had an occasion to go into some catacombs somewhere south of Rome. There were six of us sneaked off and just had time for general abso-lution and Communion. Two of the boys were killed in action shortly afterwards. I don't feel so bad about it now that I know they were prepared. Somehow or other, it seems that they sensed it.

The soldiers wear their large beaded rosaries around their necks. Many non-Catholics follow their example.

The people lived in those catacombs for the past nine months. The Nazis surely have made life hard for them. They've ransacked and plundered everything. There are very meager pickings for the Allies when they come into a liberated town.

Yes, a European tan is much more intense. You'd think we were South Sea Islanders to look at our faces and hands.

From Gerry, July 6, 1944, Italy

The invasion surely did mess up mail deliveries. The chief trouble for a while was that there wasn't any censoring being done. However, it looks as though I'll be writing regularly again for a while.

Yes, Fran, I look forward to being with you this fall. I think the Germans will quit.

When those blue spells come, just think of how happy we'll be and all the things you'll want to do when we're together again.

1944–The Front Lines

Well, I sure had a wonderful time visiting Rome for three days. Every morning I spent in Saint Peter's and the Vatican. I even was there when the Pope made a public appearance for us—and received his special medal. His smile is enchanting and his speech most consoling. The Cathedral is amazing. It'd take months to really see all there is to see. The people of Rome are so cultured, refined, and comparatively wealthy that they remind me of home.

So you couldn't go for a soldier. How about one who really saw plenty of excitement and is ready to live peacefully forever after?

I only weighed 166 pounds last week! That was with heavy combat boots and my uniform on. Two years ago I weighed 172. So how do you like that?

Pope Pius XII blesses the troops in the Vatican after the fall of Rome during World War II.

From Gerry, July 9, 1944, Italy

While I was in Rome I had some condensed milk ice cream. It made a fairly good substitute for the real stuff. I surely wish I had some now.

Please send me some Gillette Blue Blades. I'm stuck when it comes to shaving. My duffle bag with practically all my belongings has been lost, strayed, or stolen.

Receiving those Father's Day cards made me feel big. Thanks, Sweetheart. I hope to be more than a daddy to you and Mary. If I don't hurry home, she'll be thinking that Bill Pease is her daddy.

You'll have to reteach me how to dance. The only dancing I've done has been dodging bullets.

Sometimes I think I'd like to go back in the bicycle business. Then I consider a rural life. Then a stationary position. Frankly, I don't know just what I want to do after the Armistice. Guess I'll be satisfied to live my own life and not this dog's one.

The Italians are afraid, that if Germany is defeated, that the Russians will come here.

Do you remember that little brown French book I was looking at? How about slipping it into a package? It might be useful to me.

Keep your patience.

From Gerry, July 13, 1944, Italy

Here's hoping that you are receiving my mail more regularly. You might help the situation a little by sending some stationery and airmail stamps. This is all borrowed.

Tell Auntie Mary that the reason why I probably forgot her birthday, [June 13th], was that at that time I was wondering if I'd ever see another birthday.

The river incident occurred at a blown out bridge where there was a square beam and rope as a substitute. When I stepped on the wet smooth beam, my rubber soled shoe slipped and because of a heavy pack, I couldn't keep my balance. There I was, dangling from the rope, fighting a real swift current, and trying to keep all my equipment. But the worst part was, when I had taken off my shoes and socks, to find my dry socks had been stolen.

At last, my duffel bag has been located and my personal property regained. Now I can answer some antique letters I've stowed away.

When you talk about strawberry shortcake, my mouth waters. I guess that's about my favorite. Then it'd probably be blueberry pie next. But now is the time for that and here am I!

From Gerry, July 17, 1944, Italy

Guess I'll have to be hurrying up and get home before someone tries to capture our precious little bundle. It's swell to know that you're feeling so grand and are so happy with the baby.

The only thing that appeals to me is going home. What do you recommend? Well, if this doesn't end in another month, I'll be greatly disillusioned!

From Gerry, July 21, 1944, Italy

Each day makes me long to be with you all the more. If something doesn't happen pretty soon, I don't know what'll become of me or us.

Saco isn't the only place where it has been sweltering hot. I'm always in a wring of sweat. It hardly does any good to get cooled off swimming because the walk back leaves one all heated up again.

My dad writes that you and the baby are going to Quincy and spend a few days with them. That'll be swell. I hope that you'll like it.

From Gerry, July 29, 1944, Italy

Has the baby done any creeping and crawling yet? I should be home teaching her the Army style.

Gosh, but I'm concerned about your sister Mary. I thought for sure that I'd have heard by now. Certainly something must have happened. [My cousin Francis Bernard Pease was born July 21, 1944, but obviously, my dad hadn't yet received the news.]

It just doesn't seem that this war can last much longer. However, one's guess seems as good as another's. All I can think of lately is getting home to you. The days are boring and interest is dull.

I just recently returned from a three day pass. It felt swell to come and go as I pleased. Had a bed and clean sheets for two nights. What a treat!

Lately I've seen quite a number of movies. All during the shows, I find myself constantly thinking of you and getting home to you. Being away and going through all this is some penance.

Lt. Kinghorn, Lt. Trotter, and Lt. Galvin have been killed.

On pass I bumped into some of the old gang. Several have already been sent back—mostly shell shocked and with trench feet. Old "G" company really got into it.

Well, Sweetheart, keep praying. It has to end some time soon.

From Gerry, July 30, 1944, Italy

Last night I read a letter from Mrs. G.E. Colpitts. [My mother had absentmindedly written her maiden name.]

Who is she? However, I was glad to hear from her because the letter bore the news of the new arrival. Thank Heavens it was a boy. The household is way off balance now. Then again it makes it nice for the cousins. I'm proud to be an uncle. Well, Sweetheart, I'll be waiting to celebrate with you. How about a second honeymoon? We'll need one to get used to being together again. It can't be too soon to suit me. Oh well, the time will pass somehow or other.

From Gerry, August 3, 1944, Italy

Now I'm anxiously looking for those photos. After all, I haven't seen either of you all this year. And from what I hear, I'm really missing something. Bill says that you are even prettier than last year. Then again, the baby is supposed to be a happy bundle of joy.

Seeing Rome and the Pope was something wonderful. There was something very big about it all. It seems to fill one up with something indescribable. How come you never told me before that you wanted to see Rome? Are you holding out on anything else?

I'm wondering whether or not Bill is still at Devens. They should leave him there and give him some kind of an assignment. This field soldiering is too tough for men over twenty-eight—especially the infantry. Even yours truly isn't the man he used to be. Much more of this and I'll be getting my exercise in a rocking chair.

Funny how everybody over there thinks the war is won. Of course, we expect it to end soon, but in the meantime there'll be a good deal of suffering done by the boys over here.

The harvest is here. So with all the watermelons, pears, peaches, plums, etc., I'm having quite a time of it.

A place of our own would be the next thing to Heaven. It seems like a dream, but if it doesn't come about pretty quickly, I'll be a hard guy to get along with.

From Gerry, August 4, 1944, Italy

The time is going by quickly. It'll soon be September. Something had better start happening fast or else. Seems like I'll have to go in and give it the finishing touches.

We combat soldiers are supposed to get another ten dollars a month as of the time we received our combat badges. So I should have a few months retroactive coming. We'll be needing it for our little love nest. How's the bankroll growing?

How much does my little daughter weigh now? Can hardly wait to bounce her on my knee and peddle her about. I've been thinking up a lot of tricks to teach her. Have to make up for lost time. If she is anything like I was, we'll sure be in for a lot of fun. You'll be run ragged straightening up after us.

Anxious to know if Bill is still handy and if he still gets home. Isn't it swell that both he and Mary are so happy. Seems I can remember a time when both of them were pretty low. Playing Cupid was the right thing to do and fun at that.

My brother Bill is now a Staff. Jim will probably soon be. The kid brothers are really pushing the big brother aside. Guess I've reached the top rung in the ladder. Oh well, I'm getting up hopes of becoming Mister again. Being called "Daddy" will be music to my ears.

How are things going in the household? Three families must be cause for some kind of conflict. It makes me feel bad just to think that you haven't got a place of your own. That'll be the first job facing me.

Here I am lying on my back in the shade writing this. Anybody would think that this is the life of Riley, but I don't think there is any sane person who would want it.

In August, 1944, showing dad that we were saving corn for him, as he had made it clear in his letters that he was really missing it!

From Gerry, August 18, 1944, Southern France

Well here I am and still in the best of health and spirit. This is the first chance I've had to write you for some time now.

That little French book will come in handy if your package arrives sometime soon. I'd be doubly happy if only those photos would arrive soon.

The war isn't over yet, but it looks good all around, and I still have good chances of being home this fall.

This paper is plenty dirty and so am I, but only because we're not handy to water.

You probably haven't heard from me for a couple of weeks. Well, the same goes for me. I'm looking for some mail to reach me soon. My life is empty when I don't hear from you.

One German prisoner practically insisted that I accept ten dollars of his French money. The prisoners seemed to think that it wasn't any good to them.

The weather here is excellent. It's no wonder that so many tourists come here.

What a price to pay for strawberries! Gosh I hope other food commodities aren't so expensive. How are you getting along on the financial end of things?

Most of the French seem glad to see us, but some of the Germans had been here so long that they were fairly well liked.

I saw the "Song of Bernadette" and "Going My Way" some time ago. Enjoyed them much. How about you?

I was lucky enough to have a three day pass to Naples before I left Italy. I think I'll like this country better. The people seem to be more industrious and on a higher plain.

So Mary said "Da Da" before she did "Ma Ma". Ha! Ha! You must be jealous.

Keep your hopes high, Sweetheart. We're bound to see better days together.

From Gerry, August 31, 1944, France

When I said that I thought the war would be over by the fifteenth, it turned out to be only as far as Italy was concerned with me. For on that day I was one of the first ashore in a brand new invasion. I was really loaded down with a flame thrower, which I never, thank God, had to use. Since then I've had some fairly interesting experiences. But I'll save them for more appropriate occasions. The French Forces of the Interior have been a great help. They deserve much credit for the success of this campaign.

So my daughter is a "jack-in-the-box". Well it's better that way than if she were sickly or practically lifeless.

I don't have many occasions to write now because I'm too busy with the Germans. When I do write, I'm usually asked to write only one letter. So, please tell my folks that you've heard from me again. I'm waiting for the news of your visit with them.

Well, Sweetheart, I'm storing up an awful lot of affection for you.

From Gerry, September 13, 1944, France

You and I both have our troubles with interruptions while writing. It is seldom that I have the chance, and at that I am lucky if I can get one off. Now I have eleven of your last months' letters to answer.

I sure am missing all the fun of watching little Mary. Now is a most interesting time.

Who does little Francis take his liking for grub after? [Little Francis, Mary and Bill's son, was almost two months old.]

Well, if this thing doesn't end real quick, it doesn't look as though I'll get any of that corn. It looks like Christmas will be the time to hope to be home. At least I should get a good break on the demobilization. With points for parenthood, length of service, overseas service, etc. I should have a little start on most of the fellows.

Other than being terribly tired and putting up with some sorry sore feet, I'm still OK. Been doing quite a job on the enemy, but it seems as though our job is never done. I'm now sporting a German pistol. It's a handy thing to have while trying to catch a few winks on the front lines.

From Gerry, September 15, 1944, France

I'm so glad that you got to visit my folks and that you enjoyed your stay. My mother writes that you have made a wonderful mother. And that is something when it comes from a mother-in-law! Nice going, Sweetheart, you've breached what is usually considered the toughest gap.

So you are all set to have a dozen. Ha! Ha! Well, I'm hoping for more, but that many isn't likely.

137

I'm contented to know that you are able to get by OK on what the government sends each month. Don't neglect yourself anything, Fran. It doesn't pay too well. Are you getting a bond every month?

Have you weaned the baby yet? If it is as cold there as it is here, I should say that it's high time. And I know how cold Maine can be in the fall.

Hope you enjoyed "Going My Way." Too bad we couldn't have seen it together. But we'll make up for everything and it can't be too long from now. If only those Huns weren't so bullheaded stubborn! The Nazis sure keep them buffalloed. We've been actually butchering them, but they don't know enough to give up their false pride.

No, I haven't received your box yet. But I did get two from my mother.

It'll be fun teaching you to drive. We'll have to learn together. I'll be so rusty.

Don't keep me waiting much longer for more pictures.

Well, Sweetheart, I'm still OK and feeling good considering what I've been through. So, keep praying, but don't worry because it doesn't do any good. I've just got to see you sometime in 1944. Can't let a whole year go by.

From Gerry, September 24, 1944, France

My writing has been so infrequent that I'm wondering what you are thinking. Well, Fran, it's a big job we're doing and we don't have hardly any opportuni-ties for anything—even eating. This has just got to be finished up before winter and it is now the toughest going presents itself.

Gee, those snapshots of you and Mary, and Mary, Bill, and Francis are great! Gosh, I've just got to get into that group soon. I'm sure missing something.

The weather has been so wet and raw that keeping stamps or envelopes is out of the question.

You probably haven't heard from me in weeks. The same almost goes for me. Your last letter was August 31st. No, you haven't been letting me down at all. You've been doing swell. The only trouble is that Uncle Sam has a tough job to keep up with me.

The baby must be having a swell time toddling around her pen. We'll have to be getting her a bike to keep her contented.

What was the gift that you bought for my folks? [My grandparents had a September wedding an-niversary.] *It was good that you remembered, be-cause it didn't dawn on me. Yesterday was my mother's birthday and it slipped up on me before I realized it. Seems the Germans give me too much to think about.*

Forget about the Fifth Army. I haven't been in it for months.

Well, Fran, I'm still standing up under it and am living for the big Nazi crack up. Then maybe I can relax for a while.

Everybody's prayers must be doing me good be-cause God has certainly looked after me. I'll have to repay Him by looking after our family.

The picture of my mother and me that my father had been so anxious to receive. I was about six months old when it was taken.

From Gerry, September 26, 1944, France

Here are a couple of money orders for a total of $125.00. Most of it is from additional combat pay which in my case was retroactive to February. Put it away if you can. We'll be needing it to outfit that little white house with the green trimmings.

Well, Sweetheart, God is still looking after me. My health and condition are still good.

It looks to be an interesting race to Berlin. The Russians say they'll beat us there. I wonder.

From Gerry, September 27, 1944, France

This is the first time in a long time that I am writing you without having a letter of yours before me. They'd better bring me one tonight. Just think that the day is getting closer and closer when we'll not need to write! The fact that it isn't here is the griping part of it all. Oh well, it will come and then what rejoicing!

Today I marked my ballot. It doesn't seem as though my vote means much because I don't know who the men are. Are you going to vote? You should. There is talk of making it compulsory.

What would you like for your birthday and for Christmas? [My mom's birthday was December 10.]

I'm not around so I don't have any ideas. Maybe it would be better if I sent you the money and you treated yourself.

If this thing doesn't end in October, I don't think there'll be much chance of my getting home this year. That wouldn't be so good, would it? My September hopes have now long since ended.

The weather here has been miserable. It has rained practically every day and is so raw that I'm sporting long drawers.

You ought to see how proud I am showing your pictures to the fellows. I'm a real Daddy now! I'm waiting for those others that you spoke of.

Here is a formal request for a package of something good to eat. Anything will do. Field rations are the most monotonous diet. They should make the producers live on them for a while!

Well, Fran, I'm still OK and always thinking of you, so keep up your hope, and soon I'll be there to make your life complete.

From Gerry, October 6, 1944, France

Today your package arrived and I'm very grateful for it. I'm using the stationery right now and the French book will be most useful if I stay in France for a while. I've already eaten some of the figs and nuts and candy. Your choice is excellent. What a treat! Couldn't have arrived at a better time.

If this paper seems awful dirty, it is only because I haven't washed my hands for days and days. And if you could only see my beard, (through necessity be-

cause of lack of water here in the mountains), you'd know how handy those razor blades will come in.

Gosh, Sweetheart, I go big for the fancy blue paper, but it is so little a letter. It had been three weeks since I heard from you. I'm surprised that you still think that I'm in Italy and in the Fifth Army. Why it's been months since I left Italy. I was among the very first to land in southern France and have been on the go ever since.

Little Mary should be able to wall walk and creep by now. Gosh, but I'd like to be home for her birthday. You must have a circus between her and Francis. I do hope that your folks get a kick out of it all and are not bored or put out by the third generation.

Yes, I'd like to work in a garden. In fact, at one time I wanted to be a scientific farmer and go to an agricultural college. Sometimes I think I'd give it a try if I knew more about it. Possibly a semi-rural existence would be the best for us. Oh well, the future will take care of itself.

My mother writes that they wish they could see more of you and the baby.

I don't even know what I could use for Christmas. So it doesn't make any difference whether I receive anything or not. I'm still waiting word from you on what I can get or give you for your birthday and Christmas.

The fruitcake hasn't arrived yet, but I'm "sweating it out!"

No, it doesn't look like things will be cleared up by Thanksgiving, but anything can happen. So let's hope for the best.

God has been with me every second of the day every day. I've had some real close calls. Guess there are plenty of guardian angels and saints looking after me at the request of you people's prayers. Sometimes, when I think back, it makes me think of what a small part of everything we are.

Don't know when this'll be censored or mailed, but it should reach you this month.

My thoughts are always of you, and if God permits our reunion, I'm sure we will be happier because of this hardship.

From Gerry, October 16, 1944, France

Well it's been ten days since I last wrote and it wasn't until yesterday that my last letter was mailed. So this might possibly reach you before that.

Gosh, but I'm lucky right now in enjoying a three day visit to a rest camp. Finally got cleaned up with a fifty-five gallon tub of hot mineral water and those razor blades and some clean clothes. I feel like there was two tons lifted off my back.

It sure is great to relax for a while. Just eat and rest for three days. Doesn't seem possible after all I've been through.

Well, Sweetheart, I'm still in the best of health and they've managed to miss me so far. Here's hoping that they'll continue to do so.

We'd better hurry into Germany this month or this thing will last another winter and that would be worse hell! I still don't want to have to go this whole year through without seeing you and little Mary.

The folks sent me some of the snapshots of little Mary, and boy she sure looks sweet. You've sure made a hit with them. My dad tells me I've surely got some-thing to come home to.

This morning I went to Mass and received [Holy Communion]. *Going to church is a real pleasure. I've missed about four Sundays out of the last five. And to top it off, we usually get into the worst bat-tles on Sundays.*

Lately, I've been thinking much about our little place of our own. It's just got to be and soon! Can't have a growing family knocking about. I don't have any idea where it'll be. But I suppose it'll be near wher-ever I work, and that'll all depend upon what's in the offering when I reach home. So, Fran, I can't even give you a hint. Poor husband, huh! Oh well, I won't let you down. I never have, at least I can't recall doing so.

Well, I'm now sporting a Tommy gun, [a sub-ma-chine gun], *and have gone up another rung in the lad-der to Platoon guide—a job of the same rank as squad leader, but less nerve racking. I've also been Platoon Sergeant for a while. Some of the fellows who've been*

over here longer than I are getting four month furloughs, so there's still a ray of hope towards getting
home sometime or other.

I'm getting mail once in a while. I've received yours
of Sept. 6, 8, 11, 12, 15, and 17. So I can't kick. I'll try to
answer all your questions.

You'll probably be surprised in getting such a long
letter as this. I intend to write tomorrow and the next
day. So, if they don't all arrive at once, you'll have at
least two more to look for in the near future.

Tell little Mary that we'll all go on an ice cream
bender two months after we finish bending up Hitler.

The Allies are at every gateway to Germany, and
as soon as a couple give way, it'll be finis to der Fuhrer.

I was relieved to know that you finally got my August 18th letter. You must have been harboring all
kinds of thoughts. The best thing you can do is pray,
and I know that you do, so we'll just have to make our
patience endure.

You're doing swell financially, Fran. Don't scrimp. It
doesn't pay. We'll get along. I don't want you to deprive
yourself of anything that you think you should have.

How do you like the bottle nuisance? Not as con-
venient, is it? What is Pablum?

Almost everyone that I show little Mary's snapshots to, says how much she resembles me. 'Taint fair!
We'll have to have some more, so that there'll be ones
looking like you.

I can't describe how anxious I am to get home to you. My anxiety keeps growing greater every day. If it doesn't stop pretty soon, I'll be doing something drastic.

Soon it'll be time for me to eat, and a hot meal would be a real treat. Wow! I've long since sworn off seconds, and it's been keeping me slimmed down.

I'll be surprising you some day. It can't be too far away. We've stuck it out so far. A little more penance won't hurt too much. Besides, there are many thousands of others in the same fix.

In the meantime, remember that you have all my love and always will have.

From Gerry, October 17, 1944, France

Tomorrow I go back to the lines. The only good part about it is that there'll probably be some letters from you waiting for yours truly to gloat over. Gosh, Fran, if it wasn't for those precious missives, I wonder if I could keep going.

Haven't had a chance to even glimpse at that little French book yet. Besides, my mind seems too tired to grasp any of it yet awhile. Guess I'll keep it on the side until we get relieved from the fighting.

Every once in a while I bump into one of the old gang. Most of their news is of mishap to others of them. So the pleasure of seeing them is sometimes hardly worth it.

I want you to know and feel that I'll write you every chance that I get. I feel more and more what a great part of me you are. To have come over here without having you would have been like trying to swim the ocean without knowing how. And to have left you without a baby would have been like leaving you absolutely nothing. We are both most fortunate. I've something to live for, and your life is as full as can be under the circumstances.

Just think how it'll be when we are all together after so long a separation. There'll be plenty of new thrills. After all, we really never have lived together. Gosh, it'll be like starting all over again.

P.S. "Give little Mary a hug and kiss for me. She'll be able to run to the door and collect every night by the time I get to do so."

From Gerry, October 18, 1944, France

Today I'm hoping to have some letters from you awaiting me when I get back to my outfit. Without a letter to answer, I find myself also stuck for words. This rest has been just enough to make one realize how badly I need it.

I just returned from Mass at a beautiful church. That seems to be the only place where there is peace. If there is anything that I hate to do, it's miss Mass on Sunday. Unfortunately, it's been happening more so than not. It seems that we always get into trouble fighting on Sunday, and I never feel right the whole day.

There was a fellow around to see me about playing the violin in a hillbilly band. I let him take my name, but don't think anything will come out of it. Any other kind of music but that! Oh well, what's the difference.

Gosh, Sweetheart, I need you badly. I'm getting lonelier and lonelier every day. I did used to really think that I'd be home by now, but lately I don't know what to think. All we can do is hope and pray. Some one of these days everything will be OK again.

How about those other pictures you said you'd send? Oo! La! La! That's what these French say.

From Gerry, October 19, 1944, France

Dearest, dearest Frances,

I've just finished showing all my pictures of you and our little Mary to the fellows. Many favorable comments were passed and I'm sure proud to be the lucky husband and daddy.

Today there wasn't any mail, but when I got back yesterday, there were four letters from you. Oo! La! La! That's the French expression for something pretty special!

Yes, the Germans are putting up quite a battle. Wonder how long they can hold out. Here's hoping that history will repeat itself and give us another armistice in November. Anything can happen.

So my daughter is going to be a ballplayer. I'd like to see her and your father playing together with the ball.

Now Mary's practically ten months old.! Gosh, the time is ticking by. I'll have to do some fast stepping to catch up with her. Wonder what she'll think of the snow!

So our little sweetheart goes big for social affairs. I suppose she'll be having a little fun on her own birthday anniversary. What does she eat now?

My feet are in fairly good shape now, but this wet weather won't do them any good.

Well, Fran, time to sign off again. I sent you a cablegram yesterday. What did you think of it? That was the first chance I ever had to send one. [My mother received it October 30.]

Missed being paid this month. Will probably get it next month.

From Gerry, October 20, 1944, France

Here I am reading one of your letters saying that you received three from me on that day and that you wished that I were as fortunate. Well, I went you one better and received four of yours today. That's the way it goes. The latest one arrived in ten days. That ain't so bad.

Don't let the news on the radio and in the papers discourage you, Fran. It'll end one of these days. God knows the best time for that to happen.

Thanks for sending a Christmas package to my brother Bill, [in India], and another to me. You're doing a swell job, Sweetheart. Some day I hope to make it up to you.

I'd get a kick out of seeing you and Mary, [my mother's sister], *wheeling the carriages down Bradley Street. Bet it never dawned on you three years ago when you were both walking to work. Bet it didn't seem as though blowing bubbles and getting into a pen,* [a playpen, that is], *would be so much fun. Wait'll you get laughing at some of the crazy things that I'll probably do to keep peace in the family.*

Don't send that German book. I'm not the least bit interested in that language. You are right in saying that I haven't much space for anything that isn't ab-solutely necessary.

I have voted weeks ago. Hope you don't neutralize my ballot by voting the other way. But that's for you to find out. Ha! Ha!

Time to sign off again, Sweet. Some day I'll be able to do it in person. I hope! I hope! I hope! Remember how we used to write before we were married.

From Gerry, November 1, 1944, France

Here it is All Saints Day and I'm still at it over here. Oh well, it can't last forever.

This is my first letter to you in about eleven days. So don't be thinking that you've missed some in be-tween. Gosh, Sweetheart, I hate to have to go so long without writing, but it was a necessity. Sometime I'll tell you what happened to me during the last few days. Possibly you will have read about it in the news in the meantime. Anyhow, the reporter took your name and address.

CHAPTER FIVE

The Lost Battalion

THIS IS THE STORY to which my father was referring in his November 1st letter. It occurred from October 24, 1944, through October 30, 1944. My father and about 500 hundred men from the 36th Texas Division which included his 141st infantry were completely surrounded by German forces in the Vosges Mountains in France. These American forces were without food, water, and medical supplies. This hungry battle weary "Lost Battalion" suffered in this manner for five days. Finally, on October 30, American fighter bombers came to their rescue and dropped tanks carrying the desperately needed supplies. My dad saw two Germans attempting to steal the American supplies, and he fatally shot them both in order for his own men to survive.

A few days later, my paternal grandparents were at a local movie theater in Quincy, Massachusetts, where they lived and saw a newsreel featuring the Lost Battalion being rescued. They saw my father coming out of the woods dirty, bearded, and in a battle worn uniform.

According to my Uncle Joe, they went home and asked him and my Aunt Ginny to go to the theater to verify that it was my dad. They all recognized him by his gait.

My grandfather contacted the movie theater where they saw the newsreel and the manager gave him the piece of film showing my dad. The article also appeared in the local Maine newspaper.

In my mother's letter to my dad dated November 27, 1944, [a letter my dad never received], she referred to the incident:

> *The mystery is finally cleared up. That news item you spoke of was in the "Journal" tonight. I called up your folks and read it to your father. Then I talked to your mother. The headline read "Saco Sergeant Leads His Patrol on Dangerous Trip." I glanced through the write-up to see if it was anyone I knew. Imagine my surprise when I spotted your name! It's plain to see the constant danger you are in and the courage that you must have to perform your duties. I hope that my prayers give you added strength, both spiritual and physical, and that God will protect us both so that we may have a happy married life when the world is at peace again.*

Saco Sergeant Leads His Patrol On Dangerous Trip

With the 36th "Texas" Division, France.—Five hundred men were huddled together on the hilly, wooded slopes. The trapped battalion, dirty, hungry, without medical supplies or adequate ammunition, eyed leaden skies for relief. And aid came. Thunderbolt fighter - bombers reared in low, dropped belly-tanks loaded with precious food and water and radio batteries.

Staff Sgt. Gerard Cameron, Saco, Maine, First Battalion of the 141st Infantry Regiment rifle platoon sergeant, lay with a patrol in a forward position. He watched the tanks fall from his position on the crest of the hill. Then Sgt. Cameron led his patrol out into no man's land to recover the vital equipment.

One had fallen in a clearing. Warily approaching the open space from a flank, the rifleman spotted two Germans trying to make off with it. Dropping behind a tree, he opened fire with his M1. Four rounds dropped the Jerries in their tracks and secured the supplies for the men.

Sgt. Cameron, whose wife, Frances, lives on Tasker street, in Saco, joined the 36th "Texas" Division in March of 1944. He has served during the Italian campaign and the capture of Rome, and during the French campaign. He participated in the Riviera invasion.

155

From Frances, December 12, 1944, Saco, Maine

Your mother called me up last night and told me about seeing you in a Paramount news film, "The Lost Battalion." She said it was the biggest thrill she ever got out of a picture. I called the Mutual Theater this afternoon and that news film is going to be shown this coming Friday and Saturday. Theresa will go with me to see it.

The Mutual movie theater in Saco, Maine where mom saw the newsreel of the "Lost Battalion."

From Frances, December 15, 1944, Saco, Maine

[After seeing the newsreel]

I always wanted to see you in a beard, but you went by so quickly I had to stay and see you the second time. I'm so glad your mother told me about it. It was interesting to see and hear about because I know so little of what is really going on.

The Lost Battalion

I asked my Aunt Theresa if she remembered going with my mom to see the newsreel.

She said, "Oh, yes, your father was the first one to come out of the woods. He was ahead of all the others."

I asked her, "How did you know that it was him?"

She answered, "By his gait."

CHAPTER SIX

The Final Days

THE FOLLOWING LETTER is a continuation of my father's referral to "The Lost Battalion".

From Gerry, November 1, 1944, France

I'm still in good health and spirits. So everything is as good as can be expected.

Here I am with seven of your letters to answer. Sometimes I wonder if I'll ever get up even with my correspondence.

I'm still waiting for those other pictures that you said you had taken and had received.

It now looks as though I'm not going home this year. Gosh, we'll just have to keep hoping and praying. It's a good thing that you have little Mary to keep you occupied.

Well I'm now enjoying another brief rest. Really needed it this time. The enemy is getting fanatically stubborn these days. Seems that they are determined to fight 'til the bitter end.

There is a four o'clock mass and I must go. So, I'll sign off, promising to write tomorrow. Here's hoping that it won't be so cold. My fingers are practically frozen.

From Gerry, November 2, 1944, France

Here is that letter which I promised yesterday. Trouble is I haven't much time and I'll have to make it short and sweet.

Well, Sweetheart, I'm bursting with anxiety to get back with you and our little Mary. Gosh, every time someone mentions you in a letter, I almost eat my heart out. Something had better happen pretty quickly or I'll be losing my mind and trying to get home before they properly relieve me.

Just found out that I can't mail this now, so I'll put it aside and try to make a real letter out of it.

From Gerry, November 6, 1944, France
[A continuation of the letter started on the 2nd]

Here we go again. Possibly I'll get this finished off enough to get it in an envelope.

Hope you get your city water hooked up. You'll like it much better. It seems the pump has always been giving you trouble.

We're talking about dancing and I've just had some happy recollections of you. We'll have to have a record player and a little floor in our dream abode for us to dance again. It'll be some thrill holding you close again.

I'm sweating out the mail tonight. A day isn't complete unless I hear from you. There wasn't any last night. So I should hit the jackpot one of these hours.

What else can Mary say besides 'Ma Ma'? She ought to be picking up a few words. Give her big auntie, [he's referring to my Aunt Mary], strict instructions that no naughty words are spoken which can be heard in her presence.

I'm glad that the weather is finally cold enough for you. At least someone is satisfied with it. Also glad that little Mary keeps you busy and occupied. To be busy is a great remedy for being nervous about others.

Tomorrow is election day. Here's hoping that after the polls get closed, they'll get right to work on ending this mess and getting us home.

Well, Sweetheart, I haven't washed or shaved for days, so I'm going to give it a try now before it gets dark.

So, loving and missing you more than ever and ever, I'll sign off hoping for a soon occurring bright new dawn that'll rush me into your arms.

From Gerry, November 14, 1944, France

This letter writing is almost getting to be a weekly affair. Gosh, Sweetheart, I'll have to do better, but lately I just haven't been able to do so. Winter has already set in and it started off with all its effects. Even the ink won't flow very well. As it is now, this letter has to be in the mail in a few minutes. So it can't be long.

It seems that my daughter and I will be sneaking off for ice cream benders. So poor Mommie had better be getting ready for periodical days of wondering where her family is.

Well, Sweetheart, I'm still OK getting along as good as can be expected under these circumstances and always thinking of you.

From Gerry, November 15, 1944, France

Now I hope to answer many of your October letters. You've been writing faithfully and I want you to know that I really appreciate it even though I haven't been able to answer them letter for letter.

You and Auntie Mary must have quite some time running for the mailbox. She'd better not be hiding any of my letters from you or I'll be after her scalp.

Well, a year ago I was transferred away from you. Gosh, how much longer can we be separated?

Now your birthday will be coming around and possibly it'll even take this until then to arrive. So, Sweetheart, all I can do now is hope you'll be as happy as possible under the circumstances. At least I did see you for a few days while you were twenty-three. Now Bill says that you are prettier than ever. I've missed a lot.

I suppose that our little one has long since taken her first step, cut more teeth, learned more words, and put on more weight, etc., etc. Life goes on. There is no stopping.

If all I have to do is buy ice cream and steaks for my daughter, I'll have an easy life.

I suppose we'll have to get a puppy to help keep Mary contented, as well as protected from wandering too far from that little green trimmed white house.

I have sent you, through the mail clerk, one hundred dollars. This is to be used for buying yourself birthday and Christmas presents, and if there's something left, use it for Christmas shopping. I've also sent my mother twenty-five to be equally divided among those left at home. Now remember that this money is to be strictly for you and your Christmas shopping. So spend it all as freely as you wish.

Of all the luck, after carrying that French book for weeks, it has now disappeared. Oh well, I've been too busy to study more than a couple of pages. Anyhow, I should be writing home in any spare time.

I've gotten out of that bedtime snack habit. Now I eat at every opportunity because I have no fear of getting fat, and I also know very well what it is to do without. That old saying about seeing the day that you'd need wasted food really came true, only it lasted for five days!

You've got me itching for that time when we can whisper "good night" instead of writing it and thinking it so many miles away.

I found a notebook in a shelled out school. I hope the former occupants won't miss it too badly. Writing in pencil also enables me to say more faster.

Now I can just see Eleanor Roosevelt strutting around cocksure of herself now that the election is over. Some will ride the easy chair for another term. Oh well, what's the difference?

Your fruitcake finally arrived and it sure hit the spot. The next day five more packages arrived. Gosh, I suppose that another bunch will arrive at once. My mother says she had sent twelve.

Do you think little Mary will know me when she sees me? Everybody who sees her picture remarks about how much she resembles me. I'll sure be a proud daddy strutting around with her. I suppose she'll greet me with a, "Hi, there!" How will you greet me?

Things look a little brighter now. Seems that it can end if the Germans decide what's the use. The next two weeks will tell whether it will last through the winter or not.

Tomorrow I shall have to write my folks. I don't think that I've done so all month. What a crime! The days are really rolling by. The only sad part is that I had thought I'd be with you again long before this.

Got to hit the sack now. So goodnight, Sweet, and remember I'm always thinking of you and the baby. So, until we are reunited, I'm praying that God will look after you.

From Gerry, November 18, 1944, France

Here I am really craving for a package to arrive. I'm about half starved. Hungry all the time lately. Must be like a bear getting ready for winter. When they do arrive, I'll probably get an armful and not be able to cart them with me. No letter from you today, but the mail hasn't come in yet.

Today has been a fortunate one. I have a nice bed to sleep in tonight, and I'm so tired I can hardly keep awake to write this.

There is a chance that I'll get to visit Paris. That would be something and a great relaxation as well.

Just can't seem to think and put it on paper. So I'll sign off hoping to write a better letter tomorrow.

From Gerry, December 3, 1944, France

Right now, I'm enjoying a rest and am writing in a private hotel room. Some break! I'll tell you more later.

Yesterday, I bumped into Daniel Sylvester. [He was a neighbor of my mother's in Saco.] Some coincidence. He sure spoke well of you. No doubt about my getting the catch of Saco. Ha! Ha! Small world. He receives mail regularly from some girl who wears glasses, is about nineteen, and lives on Garfield Street about a block behind you.

Wow, that's some diet little Mary gets. She ought to be a superwoman.

Your package with the jar of almonds arrived in good shape and furnished me with ample nibblings for my few days rest. Thanks, Sweetheart. Mrs. Devereaux, [a neighbor of the Camerons in Quincy], made a fruitcake which also has been consumed with appreciation. Then there was also a package from my mother. Gee, when they do arrive, they come in bunches.

So we're going to be fighting about who goes to bed first. If I'm as tired then as I am now, you'll have a hard time beating me to it. Gosh, it'll all seem too good to be true. If only this mess would end soon. It'll take me a year to recuperate. But with your loving help, I guess I could rush the job along in a few weeks. I need you so much. I can hardly wait to hear you say, 'Oo! La! La!'!

Well, I received news from my brother Jim that he is here. But, our chances of seeing each other are nil. I hope he can stay out of the front lines for a while.

Gosh, I sure am missing something in not being able to watch our little one catch on to all the whys and wherefores. Wait'll we start teaming up against you. Then, what'll you do?

My eyes are burning and I guess they'll continue to do so until I see you again. Your prayers are helping me, Sweetheart, because I've had many, many close calls. God'll bring us together again and we'll have to show our appreciation by raising a fine family. Don't ever despair. Just keep on like you are.

All the love in this world,

Gerry

The Final Days

My mother's twenty-fourth birthday was December 10, 1944. On December 15, she received a Western Union telegram from my father with birthday wishes. On December 19 she received another telegram saying he had been missing in action since December 9th.

On a Sunday afternoon in late January, 1945, a taxi arrived at the Colpitts' residence with another telegram saying my father had been killed in action December 9, 1944. The household was very somber as everyone present wept.

My Uncle Joe was with my paternal grandfather when he received the news. He was in the basement of his house. Uncle Joe told me it was the only time he ever saw his father cry. My grandfather said he'd never go to church again, but he was in church the next day.

My mother, of course, was devastated. She and I traveled by train to Boston and we spent the next six weeks with my dad's family in Quincy.

Grandpa Cameron and me, February, 1945, Quincy Massachusetts

Sgt. G. E. Cameron Reported Missing In France Action

Participated In Cassino Battle

S-Sgt. Gerard E. Cameron has been reported missing in action in France since December 9, according to a telegram received by his wife, Mrs. Frances (Colpitts) Cameron, from the War Department.

S-Sgt. Cameron entered the service March 17, 1941, and received his training with the 181st Infantry. He was sent overseas with a group of replacements in January, 1944, and participated in the battle of Cassino and the siege of Rome. He was also in the invasion of Southern France.

Mrs. Cameron and her daughter, Mary, reside on Tasker street, Saco.

Killed In Action

S-Sgt. Gerard E. Cameron, son of Mr. and Mrs. William Cameron, North Quincy, Mass., who was killed in action December 9 in France, according to a telegram received from the War Department by his wife, Mrs. Francis Colpitts Cameron, Tasker street, Saco.

Gerard Cameron, Saco Sargeant, Is Killed In France

Once Reported Missing In Action

S. Sgt. Gerard E. Cameron, who was previously reported missing in action, was killed in action in France, December 9, according to a telegram from the War department, received by his wife, Mrs. Frances Colpitts Cameron, Tasker street, Saco.

S. Sgt. Cameron was born in North Quincy, Mass., the son of Mr. and Mrs. William Cameron, 318 West Squantum street, North Quincy. He was graduated from North Quincy High school in the class of 1936, and was active in sports there, being co-captain of the wrestling team and interscholastic 155-pound champion.

After graduation he became interested in bicycle racing and formed the Norfolk Cycle club, remaining as president of this club until he entered the service March 17, 1941. This club became one of the leaders in restoring bicycle racing in New England. He was well-known as a sprint rider and won the mile race trials to qualify for the national title in Chicago in 1940.

S. Sgt. Cameron received his training with the 181st Infantry and was sent overseas last January. He participated in the Italian campaign with the 5th Army until the division was withdrawn from Italy for the invasion of Southern France, and since then had been attached to the 7th Army group.

Besides his wife and parents, he is survived by a daughter, Mary; three brothers, T. Sgt. William C. Cameron, now in India, Pfc. James Cameron, now in France, and Joseph Cameron, a student at North Quincy High school; two sisters, Miss Virginia Cameron, Boston, and Marjorie, also a student at North Quincy High school.

CHAPTER SEVEN

The Letters That Came Back

My DEAR PRECIOUS MOTHER wrote to my dad almost every day. Because of the uncertainties of the time, mail delivery was slow on both ends. The troops were constantly moving and were not always in a location to send or receive mail. Mail was not always received in order of the date it was written.

All overseas mail from the military was censored. Some of my dad's letters had sections cut out of them. The men were not allowed to give any details of the war. My dad's letters were filled with questions about what was happening back home. My mom didn't dare ask many questions. She commented more than once in her letters that she hoped he wouldn't forget all that he said he would tell her about when he got home. She filled her letters with my daily progress and babyhood antics as well as all the activities of the family and neighborhood.

My mother kept my dad informed about two of her brothers who were also in the military. Paul, a younger brother, was in the Navy. Her older brother Bernard was in the Air Force. My Aunt Mary's husband Bill Pease had medical problems which kept him in the states. Their son Francis was seven months younger than I. Thus, there were two of us babies in the Colpitts' household simultaneously.

All of my mother's letters to my dad from November 16, 1944 to January 23, 1945 came back. Some were stamped "deceased" and others "missing in action." Until that final telegram, the family believed that he might have been taken prisoner.

From Frances, November 16, 1944, Saco Maine

We all got a big laugh tonight after supper. Our Mary noticed her shadow for the first time and was fighting with it. We laughed so much she went into a corner where she couldn't see her shadow. Then she peeked out to see if it was still there. She thought it was gone, but when she got out again, there it was! Every time she moved, it moved. She couldn't get over it. She had two little hair ribbons in her hair. Their shadow was what she was after. They bobbed every time she moved her head. We had so much fun watching her.

I better get started on my Christmas shopping. We were saying today the only way we'll be able to have a Christmas tree is to set it up in Mary's playpen, or we'll walk in and see her perched on a branch! I'm going to see if I can get her a doll carriage. She'll be walking by then. I think I'll get her a doll for her birthday. She loves to wheel the big carriage, and I think she could have fun with a doll size.

If only you could be with us, then we would have a really happy Christmas. We'll just have to make the best of things until we can be together. It won't be too long, if the days go by as fast as this past year has gone.

I never pray my rosary but what I think of you being with me and saying it together. It's bedtime now and time to say my rosary too, so goodnight, Sweetheart. All my love,
Frances

From Frances, November 19, 1944, Saco Maine

My brother Albert and his family were here this evening. Our Mary had a grand time playing with little Bunny, [now Father Al], in the pen. If one of them picked up a toy, the other wanted it. They would tug. I was so surprised to see Mary really pull things away from him. He was two years old in August and is quite a bit bigger than Mary, but he couldn't put anything over on her. They didn't play rough, or fight, but it was funny to watch them. With a dozen things in the pen to play with, they each wanted what the other had. Finally Caroline, [Bunny's sister], and Theresa got in the pen. Although it was rather crowded, they all seemed to be having a swell time—especially our Mary. After they went home, she kept right on playing in the pen. I guess she was glad to have everything to herself once again.

From Frances, November 21, 1944, Saco Maine

Received your letter yesterday written November first, [the letter in which he alluded to the incident of the Lost Battalion]. You certainly have aroused my curiosity. I can't imagine what could have happened. I don't listen to the news very regularly, and could very easily miss something. It seems as though someone would have heard it if it had been in the news. It is so good to hear everything is well with you. It inspires me to pray that much harder for you.

From Frances, November 22, 1944, Saco Maine

I didn't receive your bond for September or October. If I don't get them when I get my next check, I shall write and see where they got sidetracked. The others came regularly right up to September.

I had Mary sitting in her highchair by the window today watching it snow. She didn't quite know what to make of it. What a time I have chasing around after her and keeping her out of mischief. If she knows I don't want her to do something , she makes up her mind she's going to do it. If I speak crossly to her, she'll look around to see if someone will take her side. Of course my mother says, "Poor Mary," and Mary puts on a nice cry to get Grammie's sympathy!

From Frances, November 23, 1944, Saco Maine

Our Mary really celebrated Thanksgiving Day today. She had a taste of everything on the table, and did she love the dressing. We had two roast chickens, and they were grand! She had chicken gravy on her potato and she just ate everything that came her way. There was a bowl of fruit on the table. I gave her a grape to taste. Every time anyone looked at her, she pointed to the fruit. She wanted more. I even gave her a taste of mince pie.

After dinner Mary Pease sent Theresa out after ice cream. We all had a double decker—half chocolate and half vanilla. Our Mary ate about all mine and then went around begging from everyone else until it was all gone.

I can't help but think what fun you could have with her now. I think she would know you just from your picture. I have it on a table by the side of my bed. Every night and every morning she has to take her daddy and tell him a big story in her baby gibberish. She hugs and kisses it, then gives it to me to kiss, and then wants it back.

You really have Auntie Mary worried. You know how she does all our worrying for us. That something you said I might see in the news —every day she has a new idea on what it might be. Can't you give me a hint, or is it a military secret?

It doesn't seem that It's almost a year since I used to watch to see you walking through the field. With a fervent prayer that this has been a happy Thanksgiving, I'll always be your loving wife.

From Frances, November 26, 1944, Saco Maine

I received your letter of October 20 Friday. The mail really gets mixed up, doesn't it?

Whatever it was that you were driving at, [The Lost Battalion], certainly got by us. I didn't see anything in the news, but then I don't read the papers much. As long as I read the funnies, I'm satisfied. I hope I hear about it soon.

It's getting quite late and everybody has gone to bed except Mother, so I better run along. I've been dreaming too much while trying to write, and the time just didn't wait for me. I can only think of you being here with me. It's just got to be soon. It's a year this week since the 181st left Saco. Wasn't it the last day of November? It was a Monday. What a year!

From Frances, November 27, 1944, Saco Maine

The mystery is finally cleared up. That news item you spoke of was in the "Journal" tonight. I saw it just as Bill was leaving to catch the six o'clock train. I called your folks and read it to your father and then I talked to your mother. They received a letter from you today. I was glad to hear you had received more of the packages that had been sent. I was so surprised to see that item in the news. I thought that it must have been in before and I missed it. The headline read, "Saco Sergeant Leads His Patrol on Dangerous Trip". I glanced through the write-up to see if it was anyone

I knew. Imagine my surprise when I spotted your name! It's plain to see the constant danger you are in, and the courage that you must have to perform your duties. I hope that my prayers give you added strength, both spiritual and physical, and that God will protect us both so that we may have a happy married life when the world is at peace again.

From Frances, November 29, 1944, Saco Maine

Your daughter has pretty expensive taste. She loves roses, steaks, silk stockings, and furs. If she has an old silk stocking, she'll sit and play with it for the longest time. I don't know what can be so fascinating about an old silk stocking!

If anyone comes in with fur on their coat, she makes sure they pick her up. All she wants to do is feel the fur. She gets real mad when she can't have it. Mother was shortening a coat for Theresa which had a fur collar. It was a battle to see whose coat it would be the way our Mary went for it. She'll be the one to say, "Get out of here and get me some money"!!! [Mom, please!]

From Frances, November 30, 1944, Saco Maine

What a wild day this has been! It snowed last night and then it changed to rain and really poured until late this afternoon. We had our own private lake in the cellar.

But the weather couldn't affect my spirits because I received your letter of the 18th and yesterday yours of the sixth. I guess I'm in the money today. My Christmas Club check came in today's mail, too ($50). So with your $100, I ought to be able to really shop.

I hope your father likes the tie I bought him for his birthday. Won't you be glad when I can pick out your ties? Or would you rather select your own? I'm going to have to find out a lot of things about you. I don't even know what size shirt or socks you wear.

You should be here, Gerry. I just want to talk to you and look at you. You wouldn't let me sit and dream. You would ask what's on my mind. It's time for me to be dreaming anyway. It's bedtime so I better get down to earth.

You should give me some ideas for Christmas presents for your folks. They are always so good to me. I would like to give them something extra special, but I don't know just what. I better get busy. Tomorrow is the first.

From Frances, December 1, 1944, Saco Maine

You should see our Mary in her long white nighties. She looks like a little angel. Haven't you noticed pictures of Christmas morning showing a little tot coming down the stairs to see if Santa Claus had been?

Last night our Mary was quite restless. So I put her in bed with me. She was thrashing around, then lifted herself up, and looked over at me. The moon happened to be shining brightly through the window, and she could see me. She bent over and kissed me right on the lips. Then she snuggled down and went to sleep.

From Frances, December 3, 1944, Saco Maine

Bill got home again last night and has gone back. He went to see Dr. Larochelle this afternoon to get his opinion on his condition. He told Bill not to let the Army operate on him again. He himself wouldn't operate on Bill now. He says it would have to be a specialist who really knew his business. Even a specialist won't be able to make him as good as he was a year ago. He won't be able to do any heavy work. I think they ought to give him a discharge.

On December fourth, my mom went Christmas shopping and told my dad what she had bought and for whom.

From Frances, December 6, 1944, Saco Maine

I had Mary out for an hour and a half yesterday afternoon. She just wouldn't go to sleep for me. I brought her in the house and she went to sleep. A cat followed us up the street, and Mary watched every move it made.

Mary was asleep when my father came home. When she woke up, I was holding her on my lap in the kitchen. When my father walked by, she said, "Hi, Gramp". He got a big kick out of that.

Last night a little neighborhood boy was here with his sister. We were trying to get the little fellow to tell us his name, but he wouldn't say anything. I told Mary to say, "Hi, there". She said, "Hi, Tommy." (That's the little boy's name). She always says the unexpected.

From Frances, December 6, 1944, Saco Maine

Well I received a bond for October today, but I haven't any for September or November. Of course, I wouldn't receive the one for November until about the fifteenth of this month, but I should have one for September. I'll wait until then to see if I get any more.

I stopped into church for a few minutes on my way back from the dentist.

From Frances, December 7, 1944, Saco Maine

Your folks sent Mary and me some lovely birthday presents. They arrived today. So I decided to celebrate early, and opened them. [My mom went on to enumerate and describe the gifts.]

My mother had gone to Biddeford to do some shopping. She bought a little red sled for our Mary and it has steel runners. It was the last one in the store!

If only you could be home for Christmas. That would be all any of us would want. It's a year now since you were at Fort Dix. I've been hoping for a letter

from you all week, and haven't had any.
All my prayers are for your welfare.

From Frances, December 9, 1944, Saco Maine
[the day my dad was killed]

Yesterday I received your bond for September. So that is OK now.

I went to the nine o'clock Mass yesterday morning and received [Holy Communion]. *It was a dull cloudy day. Last night it rained heavily. Today is beautiful and so warm for December. I'll have to get Mary bathed and take her out for a ride in her carriage.*

From Frances, December 10, 1944, Saco Maine

Well I'm twenty-four years old today and just as much of a baby as I ever was. Auntie Mary made a four layer cake (two dark and two light) and decorated it for me. We had ice cream at dinner, and of course our Mary had some and a taste of the cake as well. I received so many nice birthday cards yesterday, but was hoping I would get a letter from you.

Our Mary is getting a lot more courage walking now, and takes a couple of steps. I don't think it will be much longer before she'll be chasing me around. She plays peek-a-boo with Theresa. When the two of them get going, it's plain to see that Theresa is the biggest baby. I have to referee and break it up when they get too rough.

From Frances, December 12, AM, 1944, Saco Maine

It looks real wintery out this morning. We had a storm during the night. It was a mixture of snow and freezing rain. The trees and wires are covered with ice. It was swell out yesterday. I went to Biddeford and fin-ished my shopping.

Your mother called me up last night and told me about seeing you in a Paramount news film "The Lost Battalion." She said it was the biggest thrill she ever got out of a picture. I'm going to find out if that has been shown here yet. I certainly would like to see it.

I received your Christmas greeting yesterday. Mother got hers too.

From Frances, December 12, PM, 1944, Saco Maine

For the past few days I've been in a weepy mood. It started Sunday, [her birthday], *at dinner when the cake was brought in and put in front of me. Ever since then I can't think of you but what my eyes fill up, and I get a lump in my throat. I guess it's the fact that the Christmas season is with us, and that's the time when we want to be with those we love. We want a peaceful world in which to live. That all seems to be so far away at this time. It's enough to make anyone feel blue.* [Was my mother sensing that something was terribly wrong?]

I called the Mutual Theater this afternoon. That news film is going to be shown this coming Friday and

Saturday. Theresa doesn't have any school Friday, so I guess I'll go with her in the afternoon.

Our Mary's teeth are bothering her again. I've been upstairs about three times since I started to write. It's almost 10:30, and everyone has gone to bed. So I better get there too. Our Mary has been pretty good since her last tooth came through, but tonight, at suppertime, she got real fussy. I rubbed her gums and she kept trying to bite me. Believe me, she can give a good bite now.

From Frances, December 14, AM, 1944, Saco Maine

It's been two weeks since I received your last letter. Oh! I did get your Christmas V-Mail greeting this week. Every time I sit down to write I try to think of what you would be doing. Maybe that's why it takes me so long to get anything down on paper.

Gee, it was cold and windy out yesterday. When I was hanging the clothes out, the wind just about blew them out of my hands, but I hung them all. Auntie Mary went out later to put her wash out. She only hung a few items and came in half frozen. So I went out and finished hanging hers. It's been the first day in a week that we could put them out. Clothes whiten out nicely when they dry outdoors, but when they dry inside, they look yellow. You can't put anything in babies' clothes to whiten them, because it will irritate their tender skin. So we dry them outside as much as we can.

Our Mary is getting to be quite a mimic. She tries to do everything she sees others doing. We really have a lot of fun with her.

My mother kept my dad posted on her two brothers Bernard and Paul who were also in the military. Bernard, who was two years older than my mom, was married and in the Air Force. He was stationed in Charlotte, North Carolina. He couldn't come home for Christmas because too many others had saved their furloughs until Christmas.

Paul, my mother's younger brother, was in the Navy and stationed in California. After living in tents, he had just been moved into barracks.

From Frances, December 14, PM, 1944, Saco Maine

You should have seen our Mary following me around all afternoon helping me. I was cleaning up the living room. I took all the pictures down, dusted the ceiling and walls, washed the pictures, and put them back. The furnace makes a lot of dust, but I wonder who makes all the little fingerprints all over the paint around the doors. I guess I'll have to wash paint tomorrow. I put Mary out in the carriage and she slept about a half hour. From then on it was a tug of war. Everything she saw me take , she wanted. Every time I closed the piano, she wanted to play it. I couldn't turn around but what she would be right in my way.

I wish it were possible for you to be with us now. I think Mary would know you right away. The way she talks to your picture and kisses it, is just too sweet for anything.

Here I am writing "goodnight" again wishing with all my heart that I could whisper it instead.

From Frances, December 15, 1944, Saco Maine

Thank you, Sweetheart, for the nice birthday greeting. I just received it this evening when I got home from the show, [in which she saw Gerry]. I always wanted to see you with a beard, but you went by so quickly that I had to stay and see you the second time. I'm so glad your mother told me about it. It was interesting to see and hear about because I know so little of what is really going on.

Our Mary is walking fine now. She gets over a threshold very carefully and keeps her balance swell. She was really stepping around this evening. I only wish you could see her. It's such a thrill to see her toddle along by herself.

From Frances, December 17, 1944, Saco Maine

I received your nice long letter Saturday that you had written the 15th of November. I wish you had time to write letters like that more often. It must have been sidetracked somewhere. The letter you wrote on the 18th I received two weeks ago.

Our Mary is traveling all over the place now under her own power. Gosh, it didn't take her long to learn once she got the hang of it.

Mother got a letter from her twin sister, my Aunt Nora, yesterday. Her son John was wounded out in the Pacific. I guess my uncle is pretty low. He really looks at things the worst way. Of course, they haven't heard any details yet, so they don't know just when it happened.

I guess you'll have to get a piano for our Mary. She always wants to play. She gets real mad when she toddles over and finds it closed.

From Frances, December 18, 1944, Saco Maine

All the mail I received today wouldn't have meant so much if I hadn't had a letter from you. I was so pleased to hear you had met someone I know. [her neighbor Daniel Sylvester] I dropped in to see his folks. They hadn't heard from him for three weeks. So they were happy to hear that you had met him. I don't know who Daniel's girlfriend can be. I'm not very well acquainted with the people up there.

I'm wondering if you will remember all the things you say you'll tell me about later. I hope so as I'm anxious to hear all about them.

I can't wait for the time to come when we will be together. So all my prayers are for your welfare and for the restoration of a just peace to this war-torn world. With every hope for these prayers to be answered soon, I'll always be your loving wife.

From Frances, December 21, 1944, Saco Maine

I haven't written for two days, but really must tonight. It's just a year ago that our Mary was born. We were apart then, but everything turned out fine for us. You arrived in time to have Christmas with us and bring us home from the hospital. You did so much to help us.

After receiving the telegram the evening of the nineteenth with the news that you have been missing since the ninth, it was only natural for me to feel pretty low. When I thought it all over and realized how good God and His blessed mother have been to us since we first met, my faith in their mercy was strengthened. I believe they will see to it that everything will be fine for us again.

I don't know whether to mail this until I hear more about you or not, but I just had to write tonight.

I called your father as soon as I received the telegram and talked with your mother too. It was about 6:45 P.M. when a taxi driver delivered the telegram. We had just finished supper. I called Father Mac, but he hasn't been well lately. I talked to Father Gosselin who came up immediately afterwards. It was so nice of him to walk way up here. It was quite cold out too! My father gave him a ride back to the rectory. I called Father Pelletier and he offered Mass the next morning for you. Father Gosselin did too. I went to Mass that morning.

Every time I get up early, our Mary has to get up too and know what is going on. That morning she was sitting in her highchair. When she saw me dressed with my hat and coat on, she said, "Go get cookie". Every time she sees me going out I tell her I'll get her some cookies. So she beat me to it that time.

Your father called tonight to see how I was taking the news. Your folks have always been wonderful to me. The most difficult part of receiving that telegram was calling them.

I made a birthday cake for our Mary today and bought some ice cream, peanuts, and candy. I had Theresa round up some neighborhood children. I dressed Mary up in a little red and white striped dress with a little red bow in her hair. She had a swell time playing with everyone. There were six children here besides little Francis Pease and our Mary.

It's bedtime now. So I'll keep right on with my prayers for you and hope we will soon be together.

From Frances, December 25, 1944, Saco Maine

It is with a most fervent prayer that I'm hoping your Christmas was as pleasant as can be in such trying times. I've been thinking of you constantly and was wishing with all my heart that you could be with us today. If only you could have seen the expression of joy and gladness on our Mary's face this morning when she saw the Christmas tree and all the presents. She couldn't take her eyes off the tree even for a few minutes. During the day, whenever we put on the tree lights, she would sit and look at it.

I'm anxiously waiting for good news and I'm praying constantly for all the things that mean so much to us. It's pretty difficult to write. I'm all right once I get started, but that is what takes the time.

From Frances, December 28, 1944, Saco Maine

We are having a real touch of winter today. It snowed heavily last night. All day long the wind has been blowing quite strong. Even though the snowplow went through the street, there is a car stuck out there now. Just a few minutes after a car goes through, the tracks are filled right up again.

Everyone has been wonderful during this time. I hope it won't be long before we'll be hearing good news about you. Everything seemed so uncertain before, but now it is more so. The only thing left is to trust in the mercy of God and implore His help to strengthen and encourage us through this period of uncertainty.

Goodnight, my sweetheart.
All the love possible,
Frances

From Frances, December 31, 1944, Saco Maine

Just a year ago today!! What does 1945 have in store for us? It's pretty hard to welcome in a new year with any gaiety, but I'm praying with all my heart that we will be reunited before another new year.

Bill went back tonight. I call him the sandman. Anytime I want Mary to go to sleep, he'll dance around with her, and she drops off in no time.

My aunt received a V-mail from my cousin John on Christmas Eve.

I guess he wasn't wounded very badly. He expects to be home the first of February. His brother Joe was home on a twenty day furlough.

If only you could be with us. I can't do a thing lately but what I'm thinking of you and wishing you were here. I'm praying that the new year will bring us peace and bring us together.

From Frances, January 2, 1944, Saco Maine

It's just two weeks tonight that I received that telegram, but it seems much longer.

When we went to Mass New Year's Day, it was terribly icy and it was raining. There was slush on top of the ice. It kept raining steadily all day. Now all the snow is gone and there are patches of ice in the fields. We had eight inches of snow just last Friday. It doesn't take long for the rain to wash it away.

Albert's wife gave me a doll carriage that they had. So I've got to get busy and paint it and dress it up for our Mary. She's always trying to wheel the baby carriage.

My sister Mary sits little Francis in his highchair now. It's so funny to watch him and our Mary sitting side by side. Everything he has, she wants. She'll take it away from him, and he doesn't mind at all. Just wait until he gets a little bigger!

I hope and pray you will soon be able to enjoy all these daily frolics with us.

From Frances, January 5, 1944, Saco Maine

It has been quite a while since I've written a V-mail, but I don't know if Mary will stay asleep long enough for me to write very much. Just as I put her to bed, the neighbor across the street started sawing wood with one of those rattle-trap machines. He has a light outside so he can see what he is doing.

I went to Biddeford today and did some shopping. Most of all, I wanted to get our Mary a pair of shoes, but they didn't have her size anywhere.

It's the first time she made a fuss about me going anywhere. She evidently thought I was just going out to the mailbox, because she didn't mind seeing me go. When I wasn't back in about five minutes, she sat right down, put her head on the floor, and cried. She got over it in a few minutes.

All my prayers are for your welfare.

From Frances, January 7, 1944, Saco Maine

I hear our neighbor's dog barking now. It's always a happy reminder of you coming home. Our Mary gets a thrill out of feeding her out of the window. We toss a bone or a piece of bread out to her once in a while. Mary just loves to sit and watch her.

Yesterday we had a letter from Paul. I had sent him a box of mixed nuts. Today is his nineteenth birthday. [My mother's brother Paul was in the Navy and stationed in California.]

Bill had a letter from Franie Martin. He got Bill's address off a letter Bill had written to you. Bill has written to him about you and we are all praying that he will be able to give us some information about you. Wherever you are, I want you to know all my love and prayers are yours, and I will be waiting to welcome you home when God sees fit to bring you back to me.

From Frances, January 11, 1944, Saco Maine

Everything seems to be going along about the same as usual. The children think up something new for us to laugh over every day. Little Francis is getting to be quite a boy now and he gets as big a kick out of our Mary's actions as she gets out of his. He thinks she is so big, and she thinks he is so little.

From Frances, January 13, 1944, Saco Maine

Our little daughter has found a chair that she can crawl up into. This morning I thought she was rather quiet. I glanced into the dining room and there she was sitting up in a chair with a bottle of ink that she had snitched off the buffet. She was trying to open the bottle and didn't like it at all when I took it away from her. I put her down on the floor and she climbed right up again. Then Mother and Auntie Mary came in and she did it again for them. When my father came home for dinner, we tried to get her to do it for him. When we were about ready to give up, she finally gave in and climbed up for him.

While Theresa and I went to confession today, Auntie Mary dressed Mary up and Grampa took her out in the sled, which has a box attached to it for her protection. He took her up and down the street a few times.

I guess she thinks the snow is ice cream. One day I made a snowball and let her touch it. She was so mad because I wouldn't let her eat it.

Bill called this morning. He isn't coming home this week-end. It's the first time he has had guard duty for quite some time.

Paul is at Camp Rousseau in California. He expects to get more training there before being shipped out. I hope so. Every day counts now.

I hope I'll be hearing from you soon, Sweetheart, and that you will receive my letters too.

From Frances, January 16, 1944, Saco Maine

I hope it won't be long before I'll be hearing from you again. I'll have your last letter all worn out from reading it over and over. It is just four weeks ago today I received the last one. I hope your courage and faith are as firm now as when you wrote that one. God has really been good to us and we must not lose faith in His divine mercy now. This is the real test. All my prayers are for your welfare and the dawn of a just and lasting peace.

From Frances, January 19, 1944, Saco Maine

Daniel Sylvester's mother had a letter from him recently. He said he met you in Paris. You managed to get there after all, didn't you? I have so many questions to ask you. I hope you'll be home soon so you can answer them for me. I probably won't be able to remember half of them.

Mother had a letter from my Aunt Nora. She had received a telephone call from John. He was outside California and was going to be sent to the Chelsea Naval Hospital.

From Frances, January 23, 1944, Saco Maine

It must be about four days since I've written. I just keep hoping from day to day that I'll hear from you and then it wouldn't be so hard to write.

Bill was home this past week-end. He was anxious to see what the Army planned on doing with him when he returned. He was supposed to have been sent to Lowell General Hospital by the 20th of this month. I think his operation is bothering him quite a bit now. He looked worried and upset this time. It was quite noticeable because he has been looking so good.

Our Mary got her first haircut yesterday. Her hair was quite long and uneven. So I just trimmed it up a bit. She looks just as sweet as ever. I'm sending a lock of her hair so you'll know it's a nice dark brown.

She insists on going out every day now, so I hope this weather lasts a while. She hums to herself while I'm pulling her along on the sled.

Today when I had her out, there was a little boy riding a big black horse. He passed us about three times. Mary couldn't take her eyes off that horse.

All my hopes and prayers are wrapped up in you. So don't you worry about us because we have our trust in God and His holy mother. They have been good to us. This trial must be for our own salvation. My love is growing with each passing day. It gives me the strength and courage that is so necessary now.

The Sunday after my mom wrote this letter, she received the final telegram, again delivered by a taxi driver, saying that my father was killed in action on December 9, 1944. The family was gathered in the Colpitts' living room. According to my Aunt Theresa, everyone wept upon receiving the sad news. After phoning my father's family, my mom retreated to her bedroom to grieve privately.

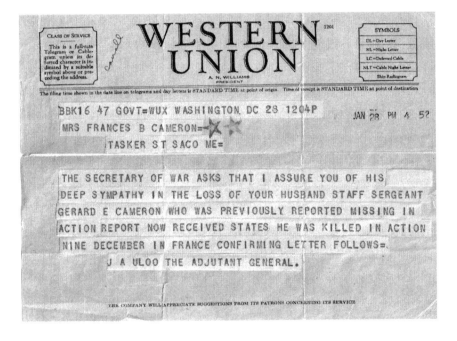

CHAPTER EIGHT

Condolences and Tributes

As is usual, when a loved one leaves this world for his or her eternal destiny, there is an outpouring of comfort, love, and sympathy to the bereaved left behind. My mother kept and left a scrapbook of such cards and letters.

The first official letters she received were confirmations of my father's death in battle. One, which came from the Office of the Chaplain of the 141st Infantry, comforted my mother with news that a Catholic Chaplain had conducted a funeral service for my father's burial and later offered a Mass on his behalf. Next, she got a letter from the headquarters of the First Service Command of the Army Service Forces in Boston, Massachusetts offering counseling and whatever assistance they could provide.

It would be months, however, before the package containing my father's personal effects arrived in Saco, Maine. After being held for a time by his unit, they were first sent to the Effects Quartermaster in Kansas City, Missouri, before being forwarded to his official designee, my mother.

195

ARMY SERVICE FORCES
HEADQUARTERS FIRST SERVICE COMMAND
BOSTON 15. MASSACHUSETTS

/ndp
17 February 1945

SPBPK 220.86

Mrs. Frances B. Cameron
Tasker Street
Saco, Maine

Dear Mrs. Cameron:

The War Department has informed me that your husband, Staff Sergeant Gerard E. Cameron, 31030719, has given his life in the performance of his duty.

It is, therefore, with deep sympathy that I address you on behalf of this Command and extend every possible comfort and assistance.

We have a grateful and lasting interest in the brave men who have given their lives and in the dependents of these heroes. The Army has made provision for you to have the benefit of our best counsel and assistance in the adjustment of your problems.

You will find the Personal Affairs Officer in your vicinity not only willing but eager to help you. The address of the officer nearest you may be located by referring to the list which I am enclosing with this letter. Should you need this service or assistance, please feel most free to use it.

I hope that the passing days will bring you comfort and a consoling pride that your husband gave his life to set men free. His name will be an honored one among all who were privileged to know him.

Most sincerely yours,

SHERMAN MILES
Major General, U. S. Army
Commnding

1 Incl.

Condolences and Tributes

The following letter from an army chaplain in Maine sums up my dad's character and was especially comforting and meaningful to my mother.

Somewhere in Brazil
March 20, 1945

Dear Frances,

Your note caught up to me almost at my journeys end, Saturday night last. Needless to tell you I was shocked at the news even though such news is more or less common these days. From the depths of my heart I offer you my condolences and I am saying mass for the repose of Gerard's soul Sunday.

It is no common place utterance when I tell you that you have lost a wonderful husband and his mother a grand boy. In our eight years in the army, I have never known a cleaner, purer, and more Catholic boy than Gerard! We often talked lengthily over many subjects in Maine, and I always left him admiring him the more.

According to our poor grief stricken human way of thinking, Gerard Cameron died before his time, too young, too good, but this is not so. He was old in virtue and goodness and in God's sight his years were ripe for Heaven. In God's presence he continues to re-member and aid all of us—his wife, his mother, his lit-tle girl, his friend. I am absolutely sincere when I feel I should pray to him and not for him.

Someday when this hellish war is over, I hope to meet you again in Saco, if so be God's holy will.

Please accept my sincere sympathy to his dear mother and dad, brothers and sisters, and all who survived him. God aid you and strengthen you to bear the sorrow He has permitted to darken your path. His holy will be done.

Sorrowfully in Christ,
John H. Clancy, S.J.

My mother received many other messages of sympathy and tributes to my father citing his exemplary service and dedication. He was honored by the military command, his country, and by the States of Massachusetts and Maine.

General Marshall
extends his deep sympathy
in your bereavement. Your husband
fought valiantly in a supreme hour
of his country's need. His memory will
live in the grateful heart of our nation

A card from General George C. Marshall,
Chief of Staff of the United States Army

In GRATEFUL MEMORY OF

Staff Sergeant Gerard E. Cameron, A.S.No. 31030719,

WHO DIED IN THE SERVICE OF HIS COUNTRY ~~AT~~

in the European Area, December 9, 1944.

HE STANDS IN THE UNBROKEN LINE OF PATRIOTS WHO HAVE DARED TO DIE

THAT FREEDOM MIGHT LIVE, AND GROW, AND INCREASE ITS BLESSINGS.

FREEDOM LIVES, AND THROUGH IT, HE LIVES--

IN A WAY THAT HUMBLES THE UNDERTAKINGS OF MOST MEN

Franklin D Roosevelt

PRESIDENT OF THE UNITED STATES OF AMERICA

LEVERETT SALTONSTALL
MASSACHUSETTS

United States Senate
WASHINGTON, D. C.

Dear Mrs. Cameron:

It grieved me deeply to learn
from our official records which have just
come from the War Department of the death
of your husband. There is nothing I can
say to lessen your sadness, but I know that
those who give their lives in this terrible
struggle are earning the everlasting
gratitude of their fellow men. For they
die, so that we who are left and our
children in the years to come will enjoy
in peace the blessings of a better world.

May I express my pride in the
sacrifice in which you so directly share
and my heartfelt sorrow for your loss.

Sincerely yours,

Leverett Saltonstall

March 9, 1945

State of Maine
Executive Department
Augusta

HORACE HILDRETH
GOVERNOR

April 6, 1945

Mrs. Gerard E. Cameron
Tasker Street
Saco, Maine

Dear Mrs. Cameron:

With deep sorrow I learned, through the
War Department, of your husband's death while
in the service of his country.

Mrs. Hildreth joins me in expressing
profound sympathy in the great loss you have
sustained.

The enclosed memorial certificate is sent
to you with the thought that it may transmit,
in a small measure, the recognition of a grateful State and its people, conscious of the
heroic sacrifice of its sons on the battlefield.

Sincerely yours,

Horace Hildreth

Horace Hildreth

HH/cw
Enc.

State of Maine

★

With Profound Sorrow the State of Maine Inscribes on its Roll of Honor the Name of

S/Sgt. Gerard E. Cameron

Who Gave His Life in the Services of His Country in World War Two.

Governor

April, 1945

The American Legion Gold Star Citation

April 4, 1945

By virtue of an act of the national executive committee of The American Legion, approved May 1, 1942, this gold star citation, emblem of devotion to the highest duty of citizenship, is awarded in the name of The American Legion, to the next of surviving kin of

S/Sgt. Gerard E. Cameron

who died while a member of the armed forces of the United States of America in the war period beginning December 7, 1941.

This death occurred in order that others might live

Edward N. Scheiberling
NATIONAL COMMANDER

ATTEST: Donald G. Glascoff
NATIONAL ADJUTANT

THIS CITATION IS PRESENTED
BY Richard E. Owen
POST, NUMBER 96
DEPARTMENT OF Maine
AS VISIBLE EVIDENCE OF ITS RESPECT
AND LASTING GRATITUDE

CHAPTER NINE

Searching for Answers

COMMUNICATION WAS VERY POOR AND SLOW IN COMING from the war zone. My family assumed my father must have been shot. However, some many weeks after his death, my mother received a small box containing his personal belongings. She observed that his wallet was singed. This aroused her curiosity as to the cause of death. So she began to write letters to the army and others seeking to find out the actual circumstances of his death in battle.

After many years and countless attempts to ascertain the truth, Mom found out that he was killed by a misfired American mortar shell, along with twenty-four other American soldiers. In those days they didn't refer to such a drastic mistake as "friendly fire" as it is so called today.

My Uncle Joe and his wife Pat visited the area where my father was killed in a valley in the Vosges Mountains. He said when he viewed the terrain, he could understand how something like that could happen.

One of the first letters my mother received in early 1945 was confirmation of my father's death from the Office of the Chaplain of the 141st Infantry. He assured her that Dad died instantly and did not suffer.

OFFICE OF THE CHAPLAIN
141st Infantry, APO 36
c/o Postmaster, New York, N. Y.

21 January 1945

Mrs. Frances B. Cameron
Tasker Street
Saco, Maine

Dear Mrs. Cameron,

It is with deep regret that I must confirm the War Department report concerning your husband, GERARD E. CAMERON, 31030719, Staff Sergeant, Company B, who was killed in action somewhere in Eastern France on 9 December 1944.

Your husband was engaged in combat with the enemy when he was fatally hit. His death occurred almost instantly so that I am sure that he suffered little, if any, pain. His body was taken to the Military Cemetery and the Catholic Chaplain there conducted the funeral service at his burial. Later I was able to offer up the Holy Sacrifice of the Mass for the repose of his soul.

Please allow me to extend my personal condolences to you in your sorrow and to assure you that my prayers are constant that eternal rest has been granted Gerard and that Almighty God, in His Mercy, will give you the strength to bear this burden of sorrow.

Sorrowfully yours,

BERNARD J. FENTON
Catholic Chaplain

Searching for Answers

The following official letter from the War Department that my mother received in 1947 offered little in additional information about my father's death. That would come six weeks later from eyewitness accounts.

WAR DEPARTMENT
THE ADJUTANT GENERAL'S OFFICE
RECORDS ADMINISTRATION CENTER
4300 GOODFELLOW BOULEVARD
ST. LOUIS 20, MISSOURI

IN REPLY
REFER TO:
AGRS-DC 201 Cameron, Gerard E.
(29 Jul 47)

7 October 1947

Mrs. Frances B. Cameron
Tasker Street
Saco, Maine

Dear Mrs. Cameron:

Reference is made to your letter addressed to the Adjutant General, Washington 25, D. C., requesting additional information regarding the death of your husband.

The casualty message received from the Commanding General of the European Theater of Operations stated only that your husband, Staff Sergeant Gerard E. Cameron, Army serial number 31 030 719, Infantry, was killed in action on 9 December 1944 in France, the same day he was previously reported missing. Additional information has now been received which confirms this report and shows that death occurred near Riquewihr, France, but unfortunately no further details were given. I am sure you will appreciate how the conditions under which our military forces operated made it extremely difficult to record complete details concerning casualties.

Permit me to extend my sincere sympathy in the great loss you have sustained.

Sincerely yours,

CHARLES D. CARLE
Colonel, AGD
Commanding

207

The letter that touched my mother's heart the most was written by dad's commanding officer who was with my father in the battle in France on the day he was killed.

From Harry G. Huberth, Jr., November 20, 1947
Scarsdale, New York

Dear Mrs. Cameron,

Unfortunately I was not able to find out your address a lot sooner. I happened to be reading though a T-Patch (36th Division Newspaper) not long ago and came across your name & your asking for information concerning Gerard.

I hesitate to bring up this subject so near the holiday season & almost three years late but I know you are anxious to have the facts, which you rightly should have had long ago.

Gerard was a Sgt. in my company and I feel that I knew him as well as I knew any of the men I fought with. I considered him the best Platoon Leader I had & at the time of his death he was in for a battlefield promotion to 2nd Lieutenant.

On the morning of the 9th of December, 1944 my company, company B, 141st Infantry was ordered along with company A to attack a hill above the towns of Sigolsheim & Bennwihr, located in the Alsace Plain, where the Rhine River flows, between the large cities of Selestat & Colmar. This was the section that was known as "The Colmar Pocket." We started out from a town called Riquewihr and advanced up the hill, B Company on the left and A Company on the right.

When we reached the top we ran into some Germans, who we had pinned down by fire & we captured them. In the process of flushing them out, we had to go over the top of the hill & Lt. Smith who was with Gerard's Platoon was killed by a sniper. After we had captured the Germans, we were in the process of reorganizing on the hill to proceed down the face to capture the town of Bennwihr, when we were subjected to a heavy barrage of artillery shells. There was very little cover on top of the hill and Gerard was killed instantly by one of the first shells. Before I could get the men off of the hill, six had been killed and twenty-three of us wounded, including myself. I was pretty close to Gerard when it happened and I know that he didn't suffer.

I had wanted to write to you after I came back from the hospital a couple of months later but due to censorship regulations & the fact that I went right back into the lines did not permit me the time. I was then wounded again & when I came back again I was put in headquarters instead of taking command of B Company again.

I depended on Gerard a great deal and missed him when I came back. He was a fine leader of men & well-respected & liked by those below and above him. His men would follow him anyplace & he never asked a man to do anything he wouldn't do himself.

209

Please forgive me Mrs. Cameron, had I known sooner that you didn't have the information I certainly would have written you.

Sincerely,
Harry G. Huberth, Jr.

P.S. if you have any questions, please write me.

When I read this letter, it left me in tears. This man was close to my father when he was killed, and he gave the family the most complete account to date about what had happened during that battle. His kind words about my dad's character and how well he was liked by all who fought with him were especially touching.

In September of 1948, Mom received final information about my father's interment in the U. S. Military Cemetery in Épinal, France. Like many of our service personnel in both World Wars I and II, he found his eternal rest alongside his friends and comrades in arms in foreign soil. A white, stone cross was erected for my dad and its precise location given for those who would visit his grave in the future to pay their respects and offer words of prayer, love, and gratitude for his service to his country.

The promise was made that the cemetery would always be beautifully maintained and cared for in perpetuity by the American Battle Monuments Commission. I can personally attest that they have kept that promise.

WAR DEPARTMENT
OFFICE OF THE QUARTERMASTER GENERAL
WASHINGTON 25, D. C.

30 September 1948

S/Sgt Gerard E. Cameron, ASN 31 030 719
Plot B, Row 22, Grave 1
Headstone: Cross
Epinal U. S. Military Cemetery

Mrs. Frances B. Cameron
Tasker Street
Saco, Maine

Dear Mrs. Cameron:

This is to inform you that the remains of your loved one have been permanently interred, as recorded above, side by side with comrades who also gave their lives for their country.

Customary military funeral services were conducted over the grave at the time of burial.

After the Department of the Army has completed all final interments, the cemetery will be transferred, as authorized by the Congress, to the care and supervision of the American Battle Monuments Commission. The Commission also will have the responsibility for permanent construction and beautification of the cemetery, including erection of the permanent headstone. The headstone will be inscribed with the name exactly as recorded above, the rank or rating where appropriate, organization, State, and date of death. Any inquiries relative to the type of headstone or the spelling of the name to be inscribed thereon, should be addressed to the American Battle Monuments Commission, the central address of which is Room 713, 1712 "G" Street, N. W., Washington 25, D. C.

While interment and beautification activities are in progress, the cemetery will not be open to visitors. However, upon completion thereof, due notice will be carried by the press.

You may rest assured that this final interment was conducted with fitting dignity and solemnity and that the grave-site will be carefully and conscientiously maintained in perpetuity by the United States Government.

Sincerely yours,

THOMAS B. LARKIN
Major General
The Quartermaster General

CHAPTER THREE

Medals and Honors

My mother's final communiqué from the War Department came in early 1949 in response to her request concerning the decorations and medals that had been awarded to my father for his service to his country in the Armed Forces during World War II.

In addition to the **Purple Heart** and **Bronze Star Medals**, my father was entitled to the following:

Good Conduct Medal

American Defense Service Medal

American Campaign Medal

European–African–Middle Eastern Campaign Medal, which includes a Bronze Arrowhead for the invasion of Southern France on August 15, 1944, and three Bronze Service Stars for battle participation in the Rome-Arno, Southern France, and Rhineland Campaigns.

World War II Victory Medal

Distinguished Unit Emblem

Medals and Honors

Bronze Star

Purple Heart

Good Conduct

American
Defense

American
Campaign

E-A-ME
Campaign

World War II
Victory

Distinguished
Unit

Sharpshooter Medal
with Rifle Bar

Medal Ribbons

CHAPTER TEN

Aftermath–My Personal Story

As I mentioned in the introduction, I grew up at a time when, in spite of many war time losses such as we had suffered, most families were intact with a mom, dad, and children. Alternately, I was raised in a household of adults —my mom, her parents, and her younger sister, my Aunt Theresa. While it was wonderful having the love of this extended family, and my Grandpa Colpitts did a

With Grammie and Grandpa Colpitts on the day of my first communion

wonderful job fulfilling the role of father figure, I really missed having my dad in my life.

Aunt Mary's husband and dad's good friend, Bill Pease, received a medical discharge in the early months of 1945. Then sometime in late winter or early spring of that year, he, Aunt Mary, and my little cousin Francis moved to the Plymouth, Massachusetts area, where Uncle Bill grew up.

Throughout my entire growing up years, Aunt Mary, Uncle Bill, and their three children spent many holidays and school vacations with us in Maine. Likewise, my mom and I visited in Plymouth.

Aunt Mary Pease holding Francis, Mom holding me

Mom and I also spent much time in Quincy, Massachusetts with my father's family.

The Cameron family loved swimming and boating. They taught me how to swim at Black Rock near Quincy. My Grandpa Cameron had a cabin cruiser named the "NOREMAC"—Cameron spelled backwards! On summer weekends the family would be cruising and fishing in Boston Harbor on the "NOREMAC."

Grandpa Cameron and me at Black Rock

We had lots of company, but I learned at a very young age to amuse and entertain myself.

There was a beautiful grove of lilac bushes on one side of my grandparents' house. The bushes were mature and almost as tall as the house. They provided a wonderful shady place to play on a hot summer day.

On one such day as I was playing alone in that spot, my father and a little girl named Sarah appeared suddenly. My father, whose face glowed from being in the presence of the Lord, told me that Sarah was my twin sister. We three played hide and seek among the lilac bushes. At that time, I was about four years old. Sarah may have been an angel. I don't know. It was a one time experience of seeing my father. I think I would have forgotten it if it were only imaginary. However, for a long time afterward, when I was playing alone, Sarah was playing with me.

This is how I saw my father that day, and how I still think of him now—with that wonderful, glowing smile!

Aftermath–My Personal Story

My mother was my security. When I was five, we were walking home from Biddeford, the twin city to my home town of Saco. My mom did not yet have her license to drive. A neighbor came along and offered us a ride. There was a ditch with water in it between the sidewalk and the street. My mom could jump it, but my legs were not long enough. In helping me across the ditch, my mom twisted her foot and broke her instep. That night my grandfather had to take my mom to the emergency room. When I saw my mom crawling up the stairs to get her purse, I got hysterical. I couldn't bear to see her suffering.

Another incident I remember was when I saw my mother's first gray hair. Again, I was about five and she twenty-eight. My grandmother told me I was silly to cry and I said, "But I don't want my mother to get old."

My mother considered raising me a top priority. She and I were blessed in that she did not have to work until I went away to college. She was there for me and was my best friend. I can remember coming home from school and enjoying homemade cookies and milk while I shared with her about my school day.

My mother was very involved in community and church organizations. I always worried about her when she was not at home. I didn't want to lose her. I feared she would be in an accident and I didn't know what I would do without her.

Supposedly, a girl develops her self-esteem from her relationship with her dad. Since I did not have a dad in my life, my self-esteem was very low. I was painfully shy and suffered intensely when I had to speak before my classmates.

As a child, I loved school and cried if we would have a snow holiday or if I were sick and had to be absent. I had wonderful teachers who were excellent role models and inspired me to want to teach. When I would come home from school, I would line up my dolls and pretend to teach them whatever I had learned in school that day.

While I was strongly attached to my mother, she was extremely protective of me. This is understandable because she had lost my dad, I was her only child, and the child of her only true love. When the boys began to call me when I was in junior high, my mom made it very clear that I was not allowed to date, that I was going to school to get an education, and that I was going to college.

When I was fourteen years old and in the eighth grade, my mom and I were visiting my paternal grandparents in Massachusetts during the Christmas holidays. When I was out of hearing distance, my grandparents asked my mom for her permission to allow them to take me to Europe with them to see my father's grave in Épinal, France. Of course, I was very excited! My mom talked to all my teachers as it would take me out of school for six weeks.

My Grandpa Cameron, with whom I was very close, was the freight manager for the steamship company the United States Lines for all of New England. His office was in Boston. Often when I visited, he would take me on board a freighter in Boston Harbor as he did his work. His company had two passenger ocean liners: the S.S. America and the S.S. United States.

Thus in March of 1958, my paternal grandparents, my father's sister Virginia, and I sailed out of New York Harbor, past the Statue of Liberty, aboard the S.S. America for the five day cruise across the Atlantic Ocean. We landed in Cobh, Ireland, the first country on our fourteen country tour of Europe. We visited my maternal grandmother's sister on her farm in Skibbereen, County Cork, and kissed the Blarney Stone at Blarney Castle before flying from Dublin to London where we spent five days. Then we crossed the English Channel by night ending in Amsterdam for our bus tour of twelve countries on the Continent. We were in Rome for Palm Sunday and were among a public audience with the Pope at St. Peter's. We ended up in Paris for Easter.

My grandmother needed to rest as she had a heart condition. So my Aunt Ginny stayed with her in Paris while my grandfather and I set out on our journey to my father's grave. We left Paris by train very early one morning around six A.M. My grandfather was relying on his high school French. We arrived in Epinal sometime between noon and 2:00P.M. during their siesta. The only place available to purchase some lunch was the train station. I will never forget that lunch as the only available drink was very strong muddy coffee. The only sandwich on the menu was a ham sandwich on very hard and chewy French bread. I remember that the ham was not lean, but loaded with fat. It was truly the worst meal of the entire trip!

My grandfather hired a taxi to take us to the American military cemetery where my dad was buried. I remember that it was eerily quiet and peaceful there nestled in a valley in the Vosges Mountains which separate France from Germany. Over 5,000 American soldiers are buried in that one cemetery— all victims of World War II. There was a memorial building in the center with an attendant on duty who looked up my dad's grave in a directory and led us directly to it. The graves are arranged symmetrically in rows. Each grave is marked with either a cross or a star of David depending upon the soldier's religion.

My grandfather's only words to me there were, "All these men gave their lives for your freedom, kid!"

Mary Cameron, eighth grade student at the Burns school, Saco, sailed March 6 from New York on the S. S. America with her grandparents, Mr. and Mrs. William D. Cameron, and her aunt, Miss Virginia E. Cameron, all of South Braintree, Mass., for a six-week tour of Europe. Among the places they plan to visit are Ireland, England, Holland, Belgium, Luxembourg, West Germany, Switzerland, Italy, Monaco and France. They will sail from Le Havre, France, on April 9 on the America, arriving in New York on April 16. Miss Cameron is the daughter of Mrs. Frances Cameron and the late Gerard Cameron. Mrs. Cameron and Miss Theresa Colpitts accompanied them to New York and had lunch aboard the ship before it sailed.

Standing at my father's grave in Épinal, France in 1958

We then had the long journey by train back to Paris. My grandfather was asleep and snoring, and not knowing how to speak French, I was fearful. Perhaps this experience prompted me years later to major in French in college.

When I returned to Maine, I was required to give a report in school of my trip. I did compose and give the report, but was very careful not to mention my visit to my dad's grave as that was too private and too painful for me, at age fourteen, to share with my classmates.

Always desiring to please my mother, I knew that my goal had to be a college education. I studied very conscientiously in high school and went on to the College of New Rochelle in New Rochelle, New York where I earned my B.A. I was extremely homesick in college, but didn't dare consider quitting.

After college I taught school as a lay missionary in Wyoming, in Colorado, and in my home state of Maine. I also had the privilege of teaching in South Korea.

It was when I was teaching in Alamosa, Colorado that I became acquainted with the Charismatic movement in the Catholic Church. I had the opportunity to make a retreat at a Pentecostal Monastery in Pecos, New Mexico where I experienced a personal encounter with my Lord and Savior Jesus Christ which changed my life forever.

One of the consequences of this experience was that my self esteem greatly improved knowing that I was a child of God. I knew without a shadow of doubt that I was loved by God.

At Last I Know My Father

In 1976 I married a precious man named Samuel Palanza who was seventeen years older than I. One day, when we were newlyweds, he came home, picked me up, and raised me up to the ceiling. I was laughing and giggling like a small child. At that moment I realized, "This is what a father does to his child!" I knew then that I had married someone who was fulfilling the role of both husband and father.

Sam and I moved to Florida. We were married for seventeen happy years until he had a fatal heart attack and left me a widow at age forty-nine. I remained a widow for twelve long years.

During nineteen years, 1985-2004, I taught first grade at Calvary Christian Academy in Ormond Beach, Florida. Sharing Jesus with my students was my passion and truly the most exciting and rewarding element of those years.

In 1991, I completed the requirements for my M.S. degree in Elementary Education. My husband Sam encouraged me in that endeavor and funded it.

In 2005 I married another wonderful man, Julio P. Betancourt. We live in semi-retirement in Port Orange, Florida.

My entire life I have hated war. My mom also hated it. She would never go to war movies or watch anything related to war on T.V. I was the same way and remain so to this day. When I was required to take history courses, I distanced myself as far as I could from the details of war.

In 2007, a year after my mother's death, I received the box of my mom's and dad's letters. In order to write this book, I felt the necessity to do some research on the European theater in World War II. What I learned that disturbed me very much was that because of the fact that the United States was fighting on both sides of the globe—the Atlantic and the Pacific—our men were not getting the supplies that they needed. This was confirmed by my dad's letters and by the information I read in books and pamphlets on his outfit.

After studying and rereading my father's letters during this project, I couldn't understand how any human person could function on the front lines for a year under such hellish conditions. No soldier should have to fight without food, water, and medical supplies, as many of them did for days at a time. God only knows how many nights they went without sleep! Cold, hungry, thirsty, dirty, tired, and lonely—how could our soldiers possibly be at their best? And yet, they found a deep inner resilience and courage that ultimately prevailed and helped spur the Allies to victory. The war in Europe ended in April, 1945—four months after my father was killed.

At age twenty-six he was worn out from bad weather conditions, lack of sleep, and lack of proper nutrition—never mind having no water for days to even wash his hands. And to be under constant danger from the enemy is unthinkable! But my father continued to be a leader and inspiration for the men in his company, and I have no doubt that he, like so many others, gave all he could to help put an end to the war.

While reading my parents' letters, I have experienced many emotions. I have a greater appreciation and understanding of my mom and how my father's death affected her life. I shed many tears as I read both of their letters.

Their faith and hope were incredibly strong and constant, and their love for each other was so intense, so pure, so sacred. The pain of their involuntary separation became very poignant, sad, and real to me. However, that huge void I had felt all my life became filled as I came to know my dad. He was a real man who loved my mom, and clearly also loved me—what a blessed gift it has been to know that! My father was a very brave and patriotic American who believed fervently in God, believed in his country and all it stood for, and loved his family unreservedly.

My gratitude is overflowing, and I can finally say with a full and healed heart, "At last I know my father!"

Made in the USA
Lexington, KY
02 November 2015